THE LITTLE BOOK OF

Leonardo da Vinci

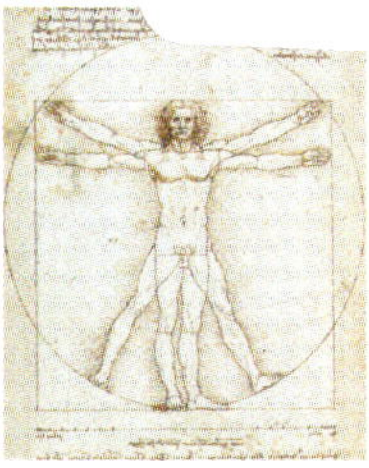

Renaud Temperini

*With great admiration
and deep appreciation, I dedicate
this book to Carlo Maria Giulini*

Flammarion

C O N T

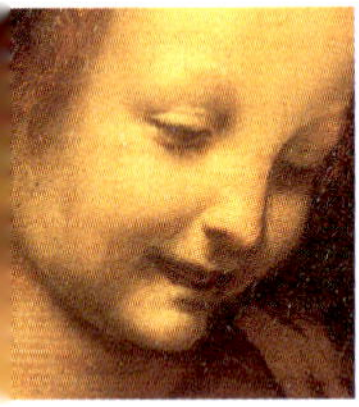

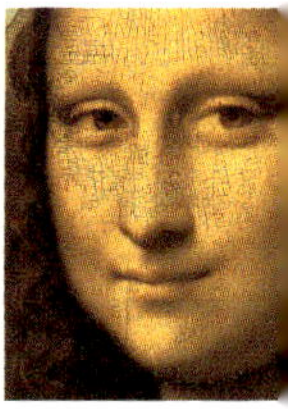

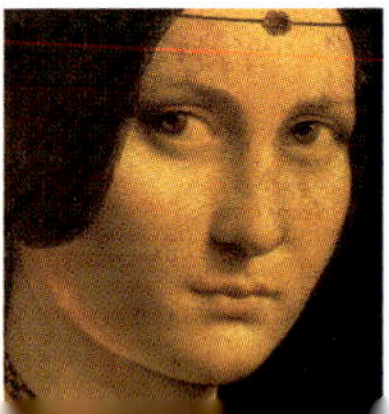

Alphabetical Guide

The alphabetical entries have been classified according to the following categories. Each category can be identified by its color code.

Works

Writings, Thought, and Technique

Historical Context

The alphabetical entries are cross-referenced throughout the text with an asterisk (*).
All works reproduced are by Leonardo da Vinci unless otherwise stated.

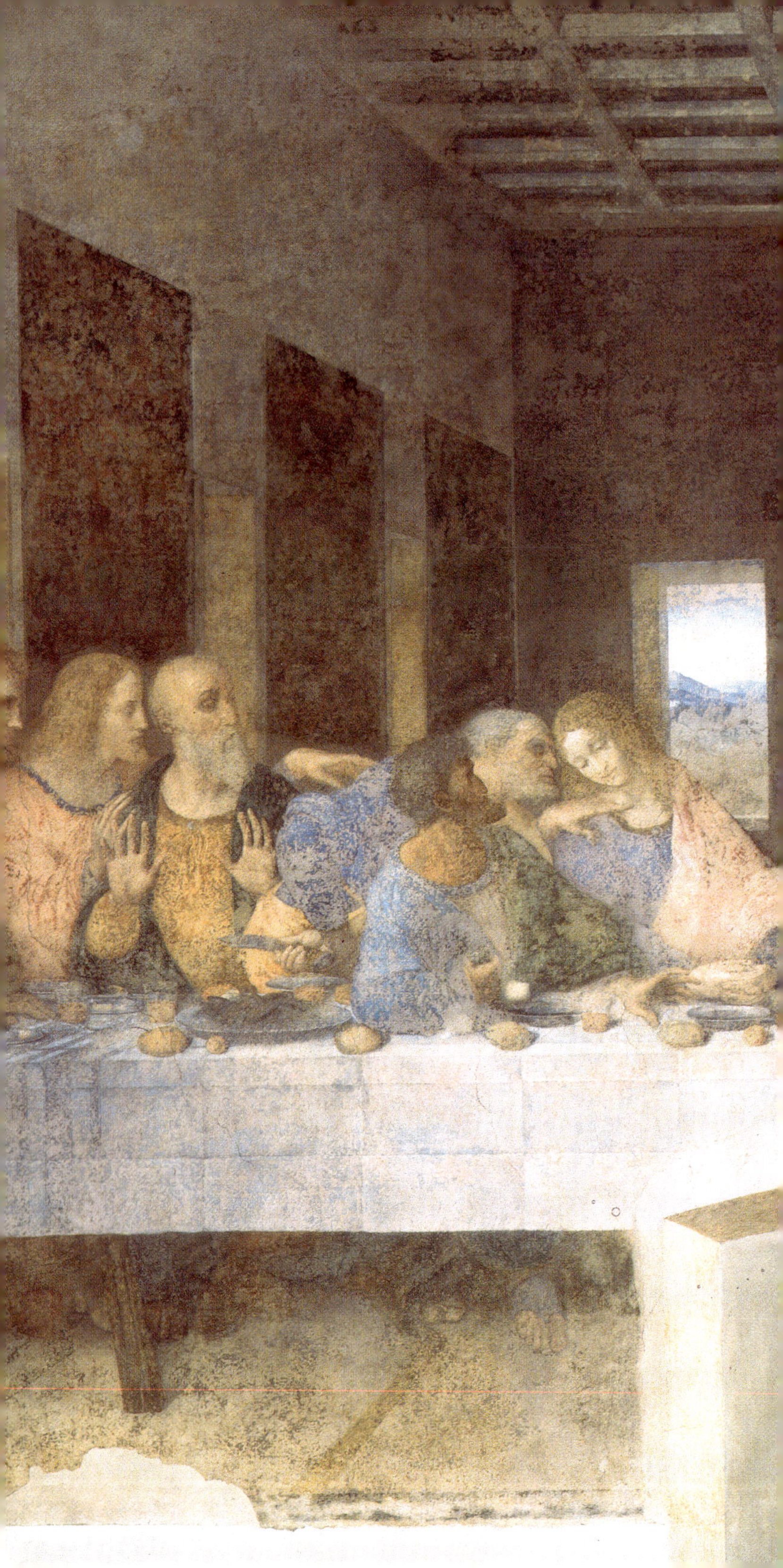

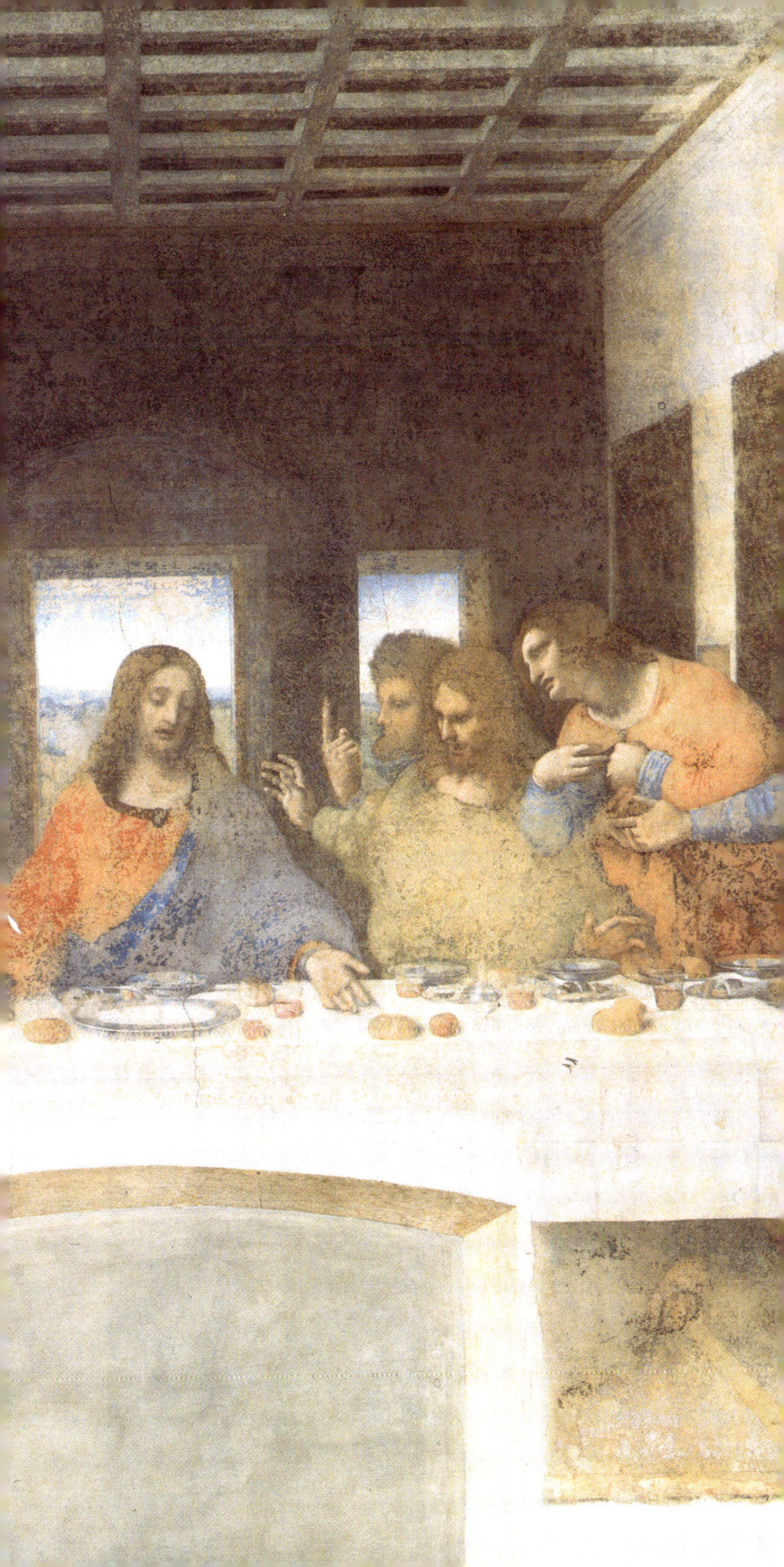

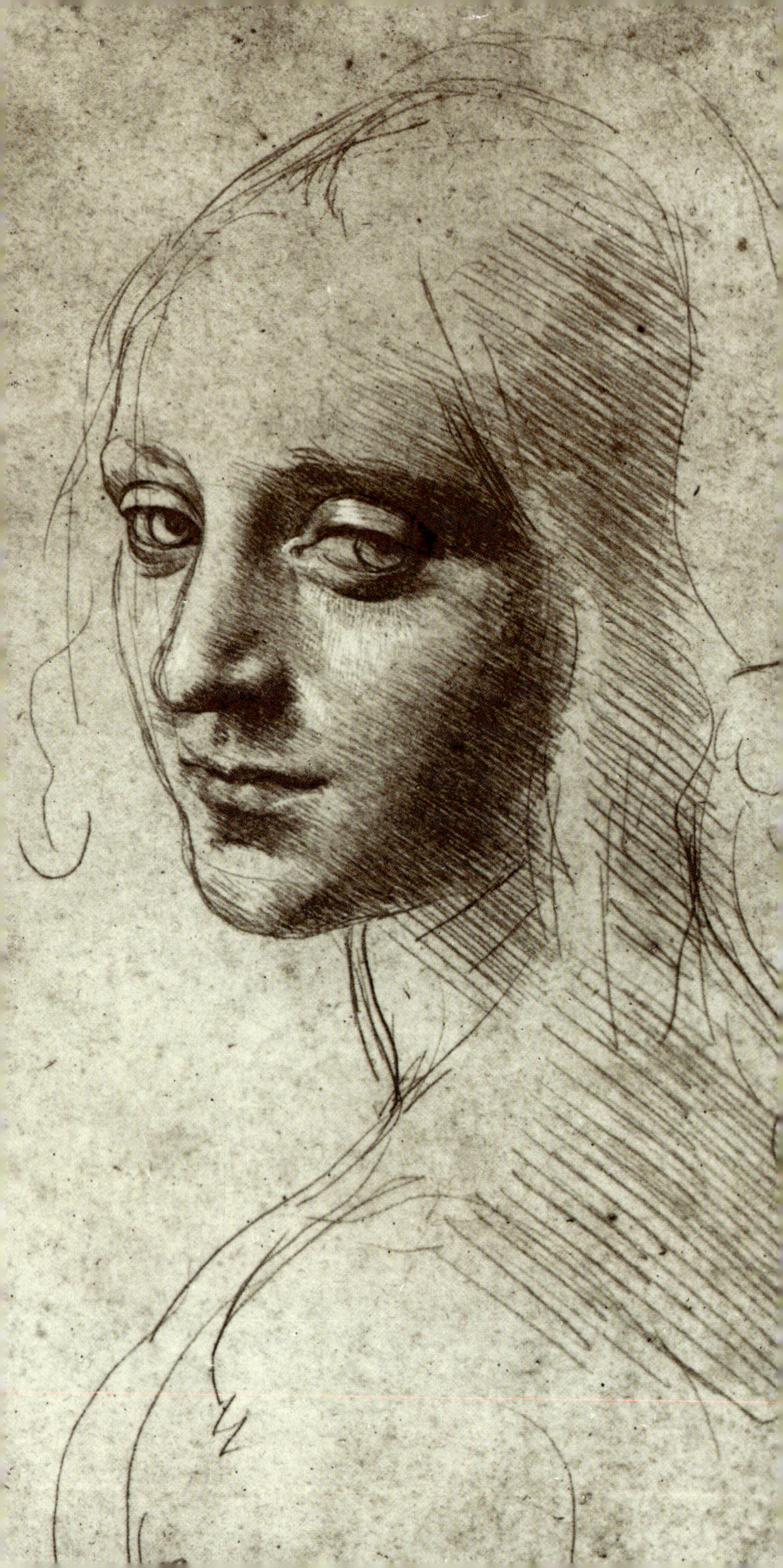

THE STORY OF LEONARDO

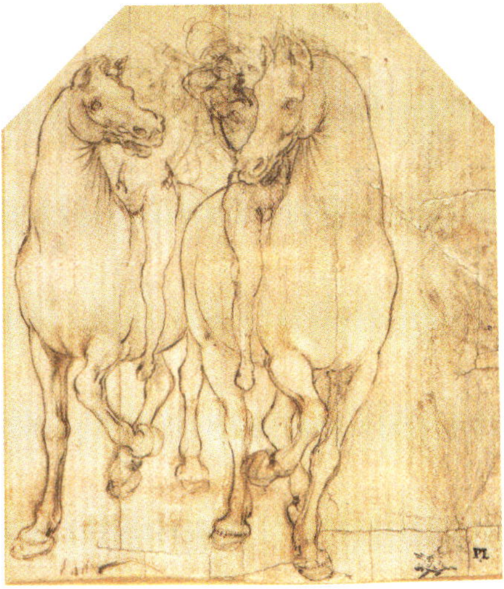

Two Horsemen. Metal point. Fitzwilliam Museum, Cambridge, England.

Early Life and First Florentine Period

Leonardo da Vinci was born in 1452 in the small village of Anchiano near the town of Vinci. He was the illegitimate son of the notary, Ser Piero da Vinci, and a peasant woman named Caterina. His diverse talents seem to have been evident from an early age, as Giorgio Vasari* notes: "Thus he began to learn arithmetic, and after a few months he had made so much progress that he used to baffle his master with the questions and problems that he raised. For a little while he attended to music, and then he very soon resolved to learn to play the lyre, for he was naturally of an elevated and refined disposition; and with this instrument he accompanied his own charming and improvised singing. All the same, for all his other enterprises Leonardo never ceased drawing* and working in relief, pursuits which best suited his temperament. Realizing this, and considering the quality of his son's intelligence, Piero one day took some of Leonardo's drawings along to Andrea del Verrocchio* (who was a close friend of his) and earnestly begged him to say whether it would be profitable for the boy to study design. Andrea was amazed to see what extraordinary beginnings Leonardo had made and he urged Piero to make him study the subject. So Piero arranged for Leonardo to enter Andrea's workshop." (Bull, I, 255–56)

Study for the angel in the *Virgin of the Rocks,* 1483. Silver point with white on rose-colored paper, 7 ⅛ × 6 ¼ in. (18.1 × 15.9 cm). Biblioteca Reale, Turin.

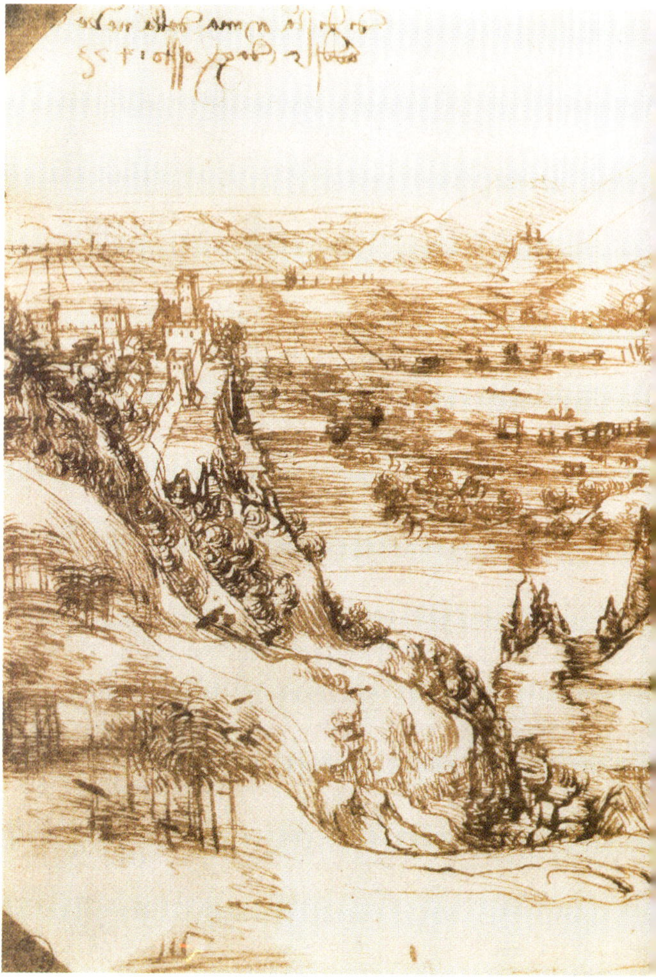

Like the other apprentice artists in the workshop, Leonardo learned how to prepare pigments, and studied drawing, perspective, the modeling of clay and bronze casting. He also compiled a repertoire of motifs furnished by his master and drew from live models. Leonardo seems not to have learned fresco techniques, and early on shunned the tempera paints typically employed in fifteenth-century Florentine workshops. He favored oil paints, a more recent Flemish invention, for their fluidity and brightness, and the transparent and atmospheric effects that could be achieved with them. It should be noted that in contrast to Verrocchio himself and most of Verrocchio's students, Leonardo was not trained as a goldsmith, and began his apprenticeship immediately as a

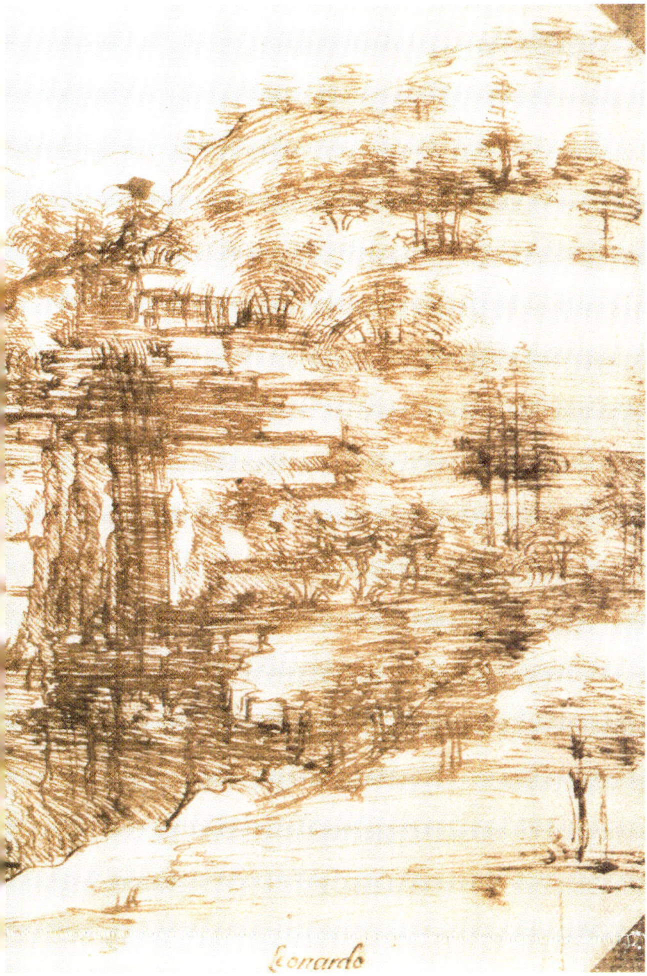

The Arno Valley, 1473. Pen and ink on paper, 7 ½ × 11 ¼ in. (19.6 × 28 cm). Galleria degli Uffizi, Gabinetto Disegni e Stampe, Florence.

sculptor and painter. This may explain why from very early in his career he attended less to the manual properties of painting, being much more concerned with its intellectual aspect (see Theory).

Although he was registered in 1472 as a painter in the Fraternity of Saint Luke, the Florence* painters' guild, Leonardo remained in Verrocchio's workshop at least until 1476. He apparently stayed on as Verrocchio's main assistant, executing paintings commissioned to his master. Vasari tells us that upon seeing Leonardo's contributions to the *Baptism of Christ,* Verrocchio gave up painting to work exclusively on sculpture. Even if the anecdote is not exactly true, it gives an indication of the division of labor in the workshop* (also known as the *bottega*).

Leonardo's earliest known work, *The Arno Valley,* is a pen and ink drawing of a landscape dated August 5, 1473 (Florence, Galleria degli Uffizi). The paintings he worked on in the 1470s are characterized by their delicacy and intimacy. The subject matter is primarily religious and includes the *Dreyfus Madonna,** the *Madonna of the Carnation,** the *Annunciation,** the *Benois Madonna,** as well as the portrait, *Ginevra Benci.** The latter bears the mark of Leonardo's personality*, while presenting stylistic affinities with Verrocchio and his best students, such as Lorenzo di Credi.

Leonardo never completed his first personal commission for an altarpiece in the San Bernardo chapel in the Palazzo Vecchio. It was eventually entrusted to Filippino Lippi. Important changes in Leonardo's style can be seen in his works from the 1480s, *Saint Jerome** and the *Adoration of the Magi,** where he expands and deepens the emotional range he seeks to depict and arouse. Here we see da Vinci minutely examining the complexities of human nature, as much from anatomical* and physiognomic* as psychological points of view. His search for visual as well as narrative truth (with a return to the Bible and the Church fathers as sources), puts him in league with the Florentine humanists while it marks out the course of his extremely personal intellectual path.

First Milanese Period (1482–99)

Lorenzo the Magnificent sent Leonardo to Milan* in 1482 to present Ludovico Sforza with a golden lyre. He stayed there for eighteen years. During that time he was conferred with an array of official and prestigious posts, from painter to sculptor, architect, city planner, civil engineer, military engineer, and organizer of official ceremonies and entertainments.* He was known to have complained about the excessive number of these duties, many of which he found tedious.

The first painting he set to work on was the *Virgin of the Rocks,** a work of extremely complex aesthetic conception and compositional execution, which was based on ideas developed during the Florentine period. Da Vinci and his sponsors for the work, the Confraternity of the Immaculate Conception, were engaged in a dispute about the painting for twenty-five years. Despite the discovery of documents pertaining to it, the precise nature of this disagreement is still a matter for specialists' speculation.

Very soon Leonardo established a workshop* with the de Predis* brothers, Giovanni Antonio Boltraffio,* Marco d'Oggiono,

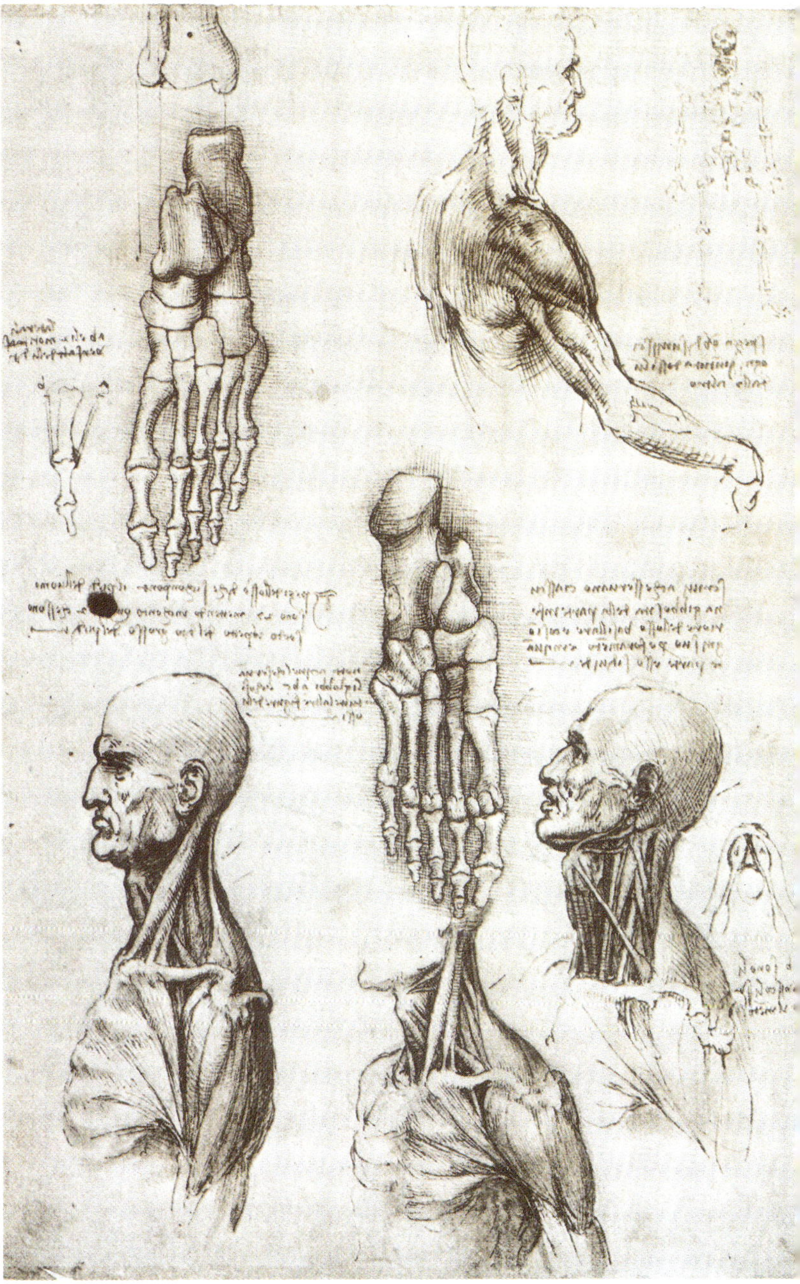

Anatomical studies: bones of the foot, muscles and tendons of the neck and shoulders, *Atlas of Anatomical Studies,* fol. 134 v. Pen, brown ink, and black chalk. Windsor Castle, Royal Library.

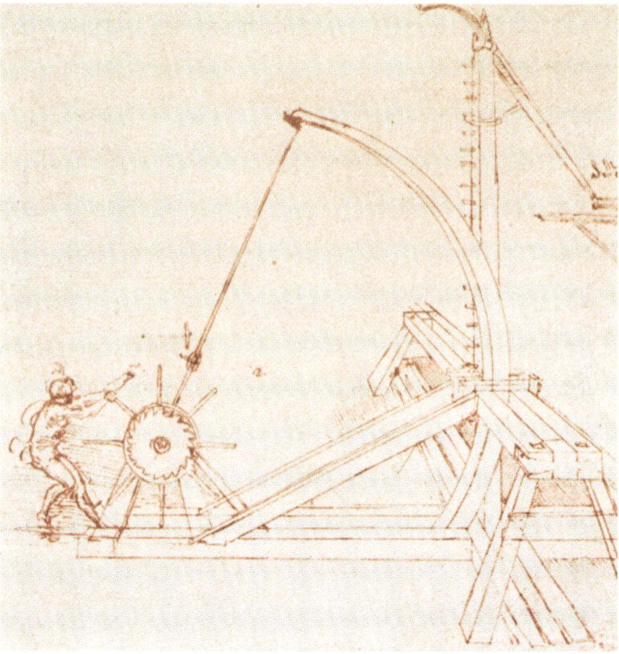

Catapult, *Codex Atlanticus,* fol. 51 r. Biblioteca Ambrosiana, Milan.

Francesco Galli, Cesare da Sesto,* Francesco Melzi,* Andrea Solario,* Bernardino Luini,* Gian Giacomo Caprotti (known as Salaì), and Giovanni Paolo Lomazzo.* Determining the extent of individual contribution to the execution of particular works, as well as determinations concerning these artists' particular tendencies and their personal output, remains difficult for scholars today.

Leonardo profoundly renewed the art of portraiture with *The Musician,* *Lady with an Ermine,** and the *Belle Ferronière,** all painted between the mid-1480s and the beginning of the 1490s. During the same period, he also worked assiduously on an enormous equestrian monument to Ludovico's father, Francesco Sforza (see Sculpture).

Leonardo's manuscripts* bear witness to the extent of his scientific pursuits and pride in applying his great intelligence to experimentation and reasoning rather than simply following the established sources of the time (see Art and Science). Mathematics increasingly occupied his attention. A keen interest in geometry became keener still when Luca Pacioli introduced Leonardo to the study of polyhedra after his arrival in Milan in 1496. The artist's study of anatomy* can be described as an endeavor to understand not only the physiological functioning of the body, but also its intrinsic essence. His technological inventions are as visionary as they are novel—for example, the flying machine (see *Codex on the Flight of Birds*), submarine, and machines designed for warfare. Leonardo's architectural* and city planning projects, particularly that for the expansion of Milan, which he developed with Bramante,* are based on a synthesis of rational organization, functionality, aesthetics, and symbolism.

The performing arts of theater and court entertainments* provided opportunities for Leonardo to put his mechanical and automated inventions and scenic apparatuses to work, while giving free rein to his taste for humor and brilliant strokes of inspiration. An analogous, playful spirit is discerned in the precision and detail of his extraordinary drawings of mechanical looms and clocks. These provided him opportunity to study the laws underlying physical mechanics, the way weights and other objects move and come to rest in breathtaking demonstrations of the balance and continuity between universal scientific principles and particular materials and functions. But his technical and scientific research was always a sort of preliminary investigation and preparation for his painting. When Ludovico Sforza commissioned the painting of the *Last Supper** for the refectory of Santa Maria delle Grazie, in which the duke was building a family mausoleum, Leonardo finally found the opportunity to concentrate, into one

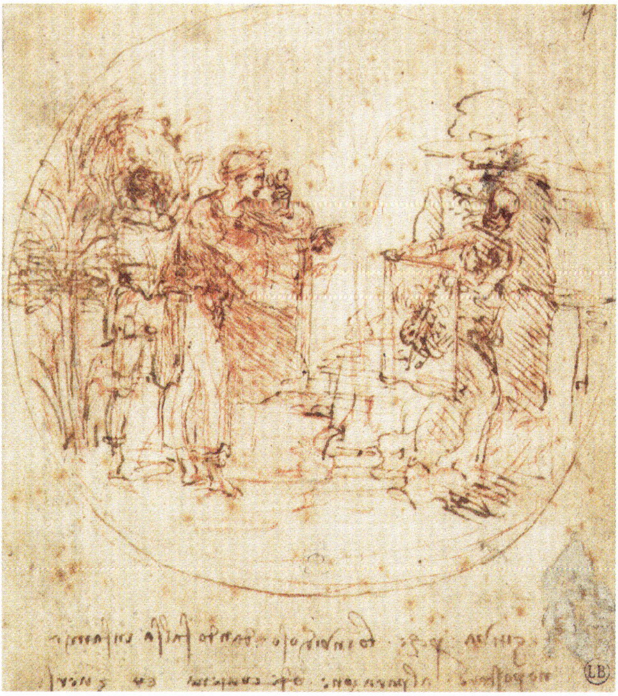

Allegorical subject. Pen, brown ink, and red chalk on beige paper. Musée Bonnat, Bayonne.

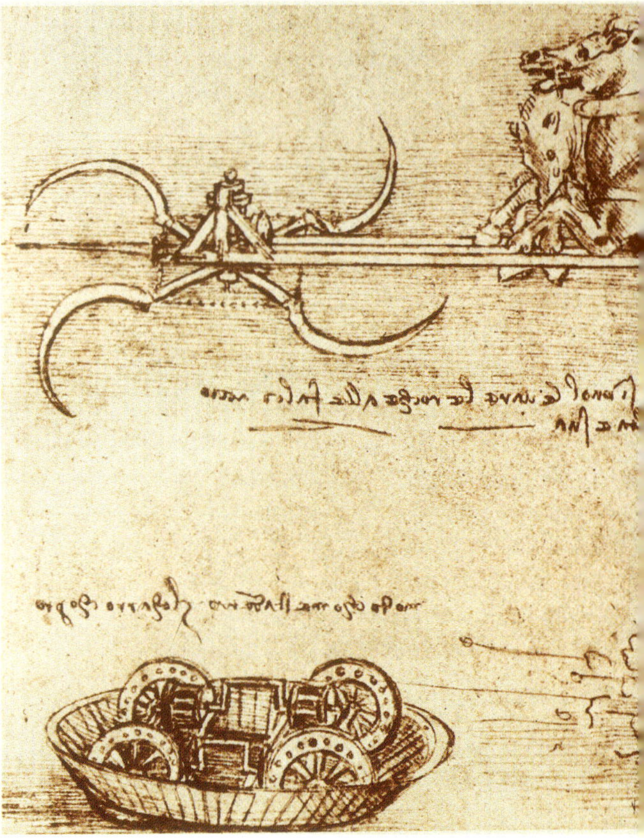

project, the range of scientific and artistic activity that he had been engaged in since his Florentine days. Enthusiasm for the work was immediate, intense, and persistent. Louis XII, Francis I, and even Napoleon, attempted in vain to have the painting—including the wall upon which it was painted—brought to the kingdom of France.

From 1495 to 1498 Leonardo worked on the wall, ceiling, and vault decorations of the Saletta Negra and Sala delle Asse* rooms in the Castello Sforzesco. Beautifully intricate intertwining tree branches and family symbols are painted into allegorical and trompe l'oeil architecture.

Second Florentine Period (1500–08)

Leonardo left Milan in December 1499, after the invasion of Milan and the defeat of Ludovico Sforza at the hands of France's King Louis XII. Before returning to Florence, he spent some time

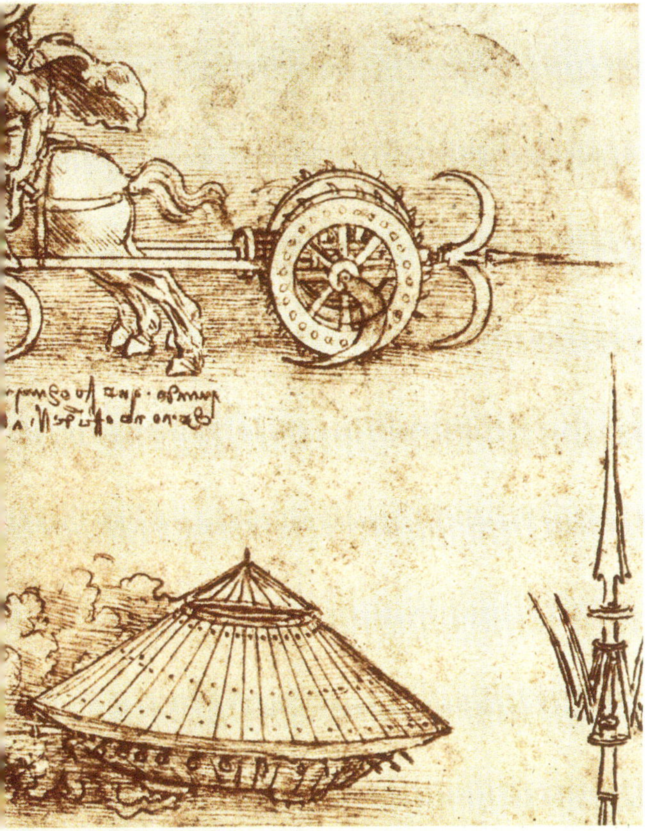

War machines. Pen and ink on paper. British Museum, London.

in northern Italy.* In Mantua, he made a pastel portrait of Isabella d'Este* and she often—apparently in vain—requested him to paint other works for her. When he stayed briefly in Venice* in early 1500, he considerably influenced* young painters there, particularly Giorgione and Titian.

Florence had changed considerably during Leonardo's eighteen-year absence. The Medici had been driven out of the city and the republican government was engaged in a seemingly endless war against Pisa. Leonardo was called upon to contribute as a military engineer.

Among his always multiple activities, Leonardo apparently enjoyed the role of counselor at this time. His advice was sought on public and private architectural projects as well as on the purchase of works of art. Correspondence between Isabella d'Este and her Florentine confidants reveal that during this time, Leonardo's lifestyle was "so unstable and uncertain it might be said he lives from day to day," that "he sometimes lent a hand to some of the portraits his students were painting," and that "he worked ardently at geometry," but it that he was "exasperated with the paintbrush."

In 1502 Leonardo entered into the service of Cesar Borgia as a military engineer, designing fortification plans and deadly war machines as he followed Borgia in campaigns through Emilia-Romana, the Marches, Umbria, and Tuscany. Notes concerning this itinerary can be seen in the Codices* of the Institut de France (*Codex L*).

Continuing a project he had begun in Lombardy, he perfected urban planning and hydrology techniques, most notably in his ambitious plan to divert the Arno River (as seen in the *Codex Leister**). The Arno project, with its military, agricultural, and commercial applications, was started in 1504 but turned out to be a tremendous failure.

In October 1503, the Florentine government commissioned Leonardo to do a wall painting of the *Battle of Anghiari* for the Salone dei Cinquecento in the Palazzo Vecchio. Michelangelo, with whom Leonardo was on very poor terms, was commissioned to paint a *Battle of Cascina* on the opposite wall. Leonardo abandoned the usual fresco technique to try a new approach of his own devising. Tradition has it that an unfortunate experiment led to the ruin of a portion of the work: torches brought in to dry the surface of the wall caused the unstable colors to disintegrate. In the 1550s Vasari* was called upon to redecorate the very same room, and all that now remains of the *Battle of Anghiari* are preparatory drawings and old copies dating to the period.

Study for the *Battle of Anghiari*, c. 1504–06.
Pen and ink on paper, 6 ¼ × 6 ⅛ in. (16.5 × 15.3 cm).
Galleria dell'Accademia, Venice.

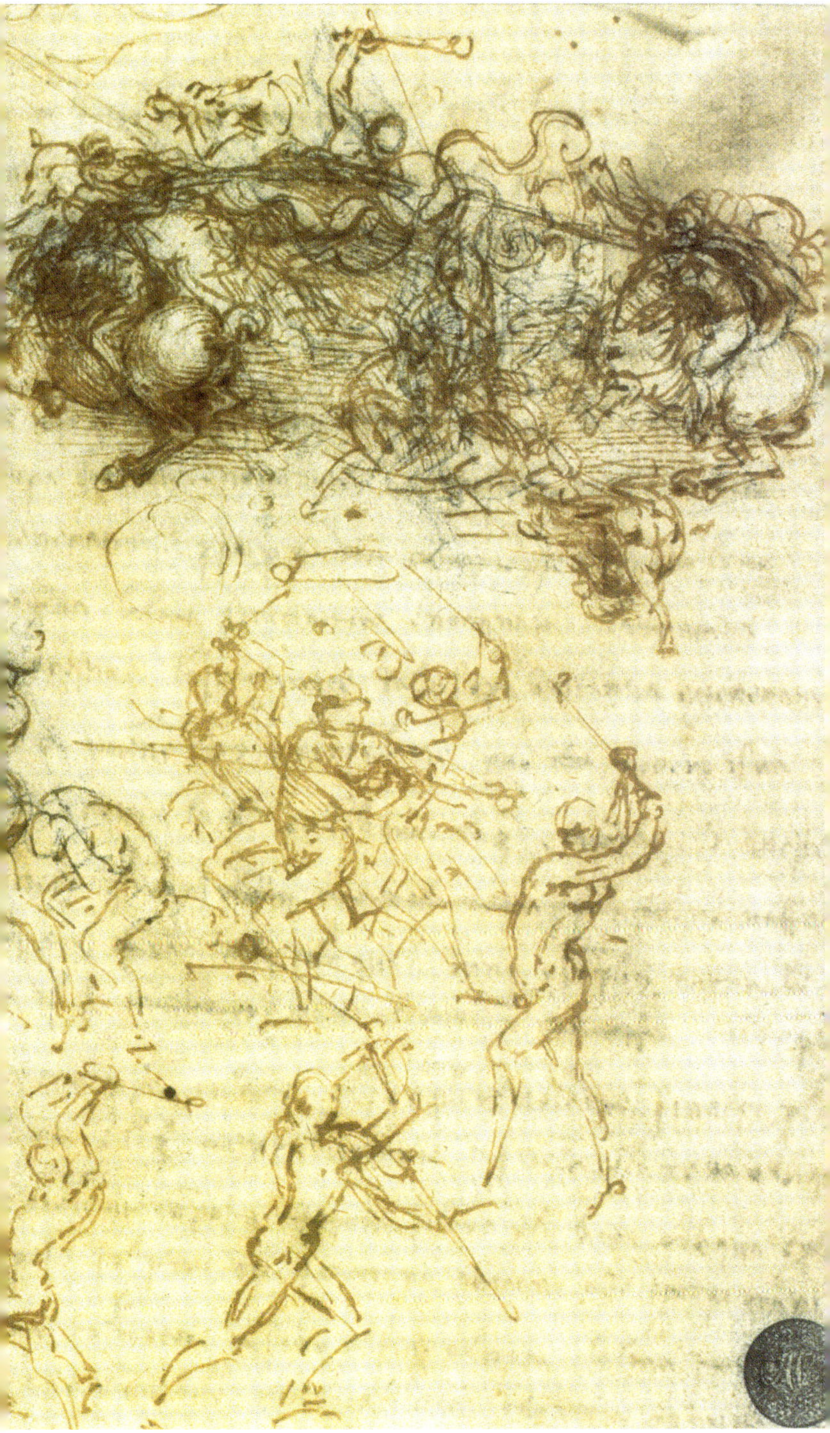

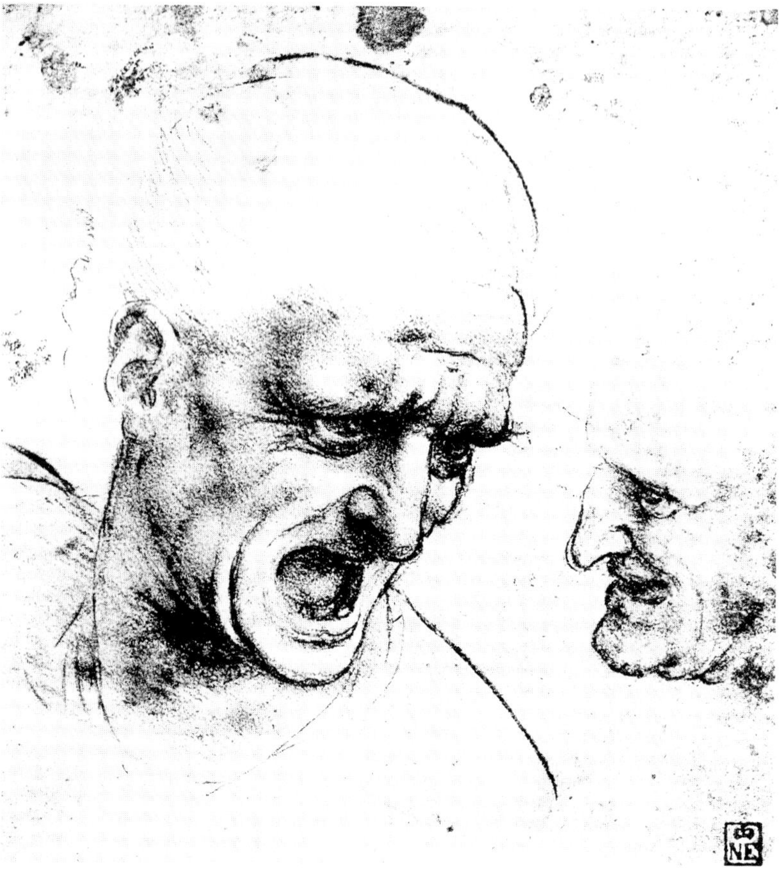

Study for the *Battle of Anghiari*, c. 1504–06. Metal point, brown ink, and chalk. Szépmüsvézeti Muzeum, Budapest.

Artistic production from the second Florentine period includes the *Burlington House Cartoon,** the *Mona Lisa,* La Scapiliata,** and *Leda and the Swan*. The latter is lost, but preliminary studies for it as well as workshop* versions and a Raphael drawing (Windsor Castle, Royal Library), still give some indication of what it may have been like.

Beginning in 1505, both the Florentine government and the French government (installed in Milan) sought to employ Leonardo on a permanent basis—and to retain him to complete works already underway. The result was that he traveled between Tuscany and Lombardy for several years.

Second Milanese Period (1508–13)

In September 1508, Leonardo left Florence* for the last time. New areas of reflection and research presented themselves in Milan.*

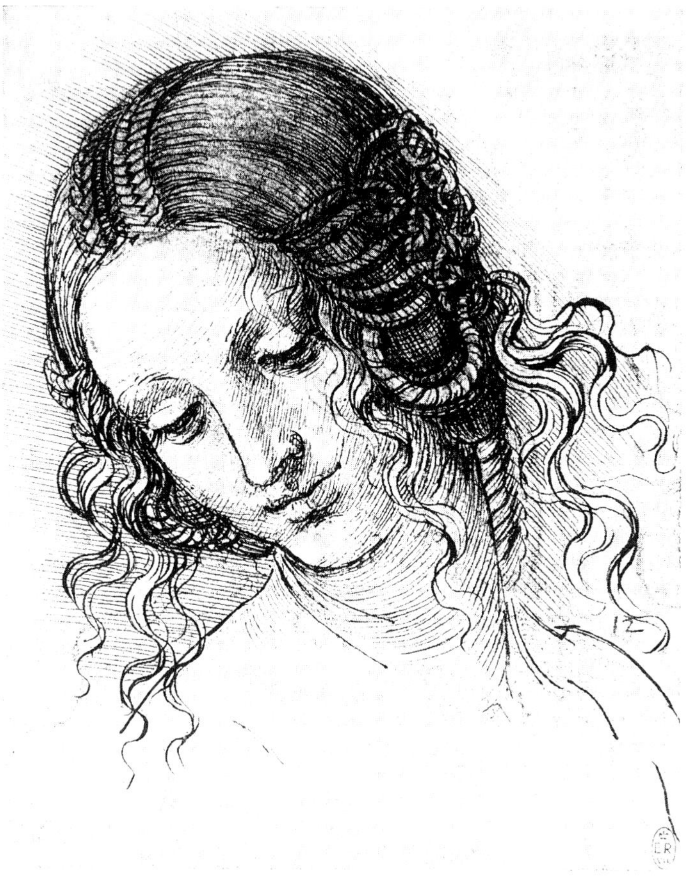

Study for *Leda and the Swan,* 1513–16. Pen and ink on paper. Windsor Castle, Royal Library.

Manuscripts* from the period indicate his intense interest in optics (see *Sfumato*) and his quest to uncover the scientific laws behind vision. Meanwhile he in no way abandoned his research in astronomy, geology, hydraulics, and the flight of birds. His obsession with water and waterways continued, as the *Codex Leister** attests, and led to his elaboration of a veritable hydraulic cartography of Lombardy. He conceived of daring projects for dams and covered canals, for example, making the Adda River navigable.

Leonardo's study of mechanical dynamics, weight, movement, and inertia led to his conceiving of an equilibrium to the universe based on the harmony of proportions, which he endeavored to apply in all the arts, from music to painting, to sculpture,* to architecture.*

He designed a villa and grounds for Charles d'Amboise with a number of fantastic special effects. These included fountains with complex mechanical movements, hydraulic mills powering musical instruments and an immense automatic clock, as well as inventions mixing artifice and nature, such as an almost invisible leather lattice for keeping all sorts of birds.

Leonardo also worked in Milan on a funerary monument for Gian Giacomo Trivulzio, the Italian commander of the French forces who captured the duchy for the French in 1499. The monument was never built. But examination of Leonardo's preliminary studies reveal similarities to Michelangelo's tomb for Pope Julius II in Rome.*

Around 1510 Leonardo worked on a series of in-depth anatomical studies: His desire to represent three dimensions as accurately as possible led him to approach the same organ or muscle from several perspectives, thereby allying the precision of the vivisectionist with the incomparable figurative quality of the artist.

During the second Milanese period, Leonardo's pictorial output was less abundant than that of his first stay. It mainly includes paintings that he continued to work on after leaving the city, notably *Saint John the Baptist,* *Virgin and Child with Saint Anne and a Lamb,** and *Bacchus/Saint John the Baptist.* *

Rome and Amboise (1513–19)

In 1513, Massimiliano Sforza, Ludovico's son, was installed as duke when the French were ousted from Milan.* Despite his earlier links with the Sforza, family, Leonardo was considered too much of an ally of the king of France,* and so he took refuge in Rome.* His protector there, Cardinal Giuliano de' Medici, provided him with a workshop* in the Belvedere of the Vatican. There he met up with the musician Atalante Migliorotti, who was involved in overseeing construction at Saint Peter's Basilica, as well as with other friends and disciples, including Bramante* and Cesare da Sesto.*

Leonardo's interest in ancient ruins and statuary were keen at the time, as can be seen in the *Burlington House Cartoon** and the *Virgin and Child with Saint Anne and a Lamb** in the Louvre. His aesthetic, scientific, and technical research continued, as evidenced in drawings* of machines for working metals and minting coins, or in impressive drawings of volumetric figures and complex interlocking geometric arrangements with sophisticated mechanical applications.

In a completely different domain, Leonardo entertained his hosts by organizing events for the court, often using animals. Vasari* describes how he "disguised" a live lizard as a monster

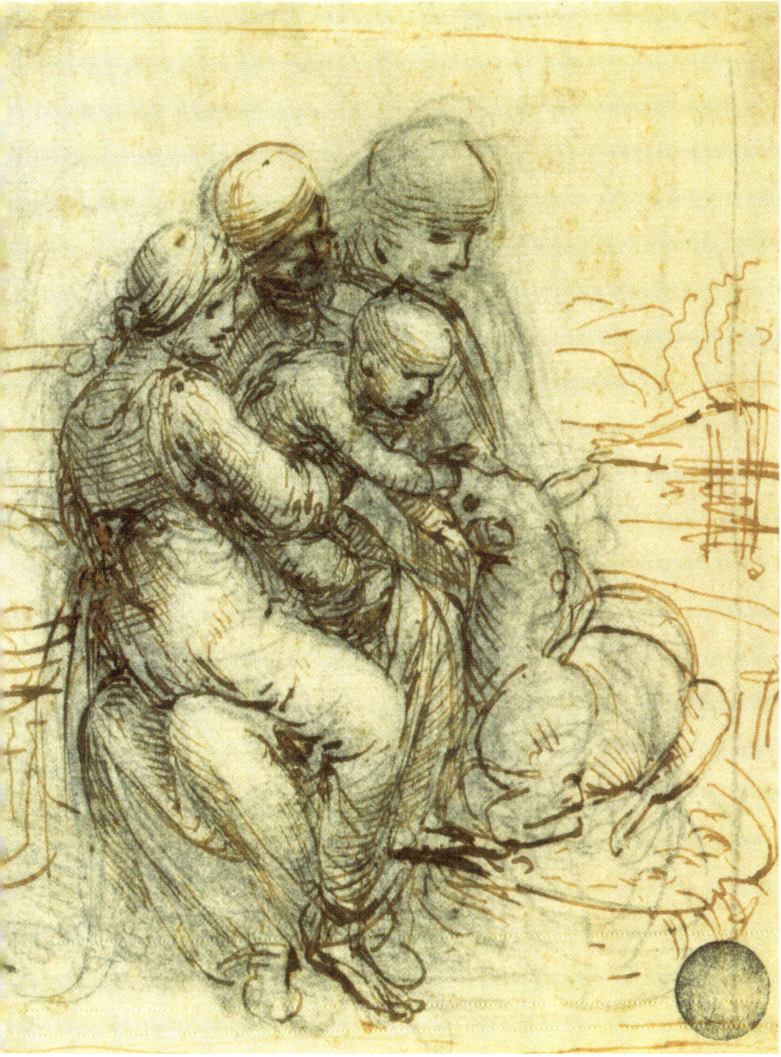

Study for the *Virgin and Child with Saint Anne and a Lamb.* Pen and ink on paper. Galleria dell'Accademia, Venice.

using quicksilver and scales, and that he enjoyed modeling animal figurines in wax which he then launched into the air by blowing into them. But even these apparently trivial activities were really practical applications of his theoretical* investigations. In Leonardo's hands a straw for blowing bubbles became a means for testing principles of fluid mechanics.

Although he lived in Rome, Leonardo traveled to northern and central Italy as well. Giuliano de' Medici was named lieutenant general of the pontifical armies and Leonardo accompanied him on an inspection tour in 1514. In Florence, he drew up plans

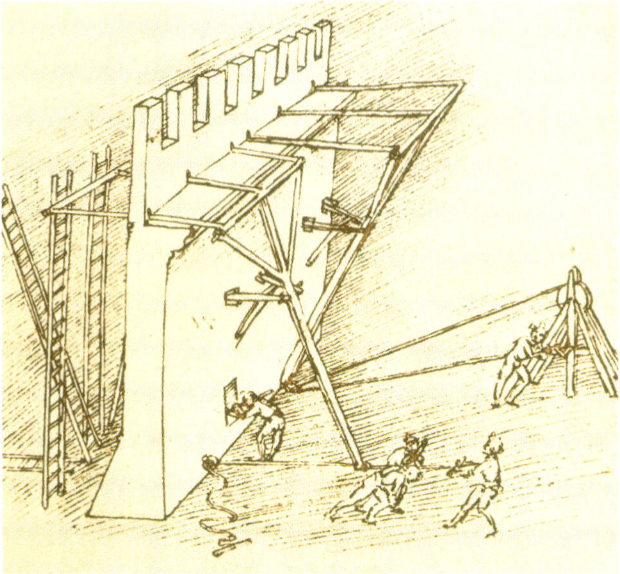

Assault ladder, *Codex Atlanticus,* fol. 49 v. Biblioteca Ambrosiana, Milan.

for a new Medici palace, and in 1515, he met Francis I of France in Bologna.

A number of notes from 1516 indicate that Leonardo experienced moments of difficulty and discouragement. We find him complaining about the lack of assiduity of his assistants Giorgio Tedesco and Giovanni degli Specchi, and accusing them of surreptitiously working for others. His relationship with the Pope also deteriorated because of accusations that he dissected cadavers for his anatomical* studies. He wrote at the time, "the Medicis [or perhaps the medical doctors, the word is the same in Italian] created me and now they are destroying me." (*Codex Atlanticus,** 159 r.)

But after the death of Louis XII in 1514, then that of Giuliano de' Medici in 1516, Leonardo found an enthusiastic sponsor in France's new king, Francis I. He was named First Painter to the King and was invited to Cloux, near Amboise, where he lived out the rest of his days.

He again took up the construction of sets for court entertainments,* and even reproduced his famous *Mechanical Lion* in honor of the king on June 17, 1518. As First Engineer and Architect* to the King, he designed a spectacular royal residence at Romorantin. It was never built, but the coherency of its conception must have excited French architects of the time.

When Cardinal Luigi d'Aragona visited Leonardo in October 1517, his secretary, Antonio De Beatis, took down precious information concerning Leonardo's manuscripts,* including details about the great master's desire to organize and publish them (which he never managed to do), about his health (he was suffering from "paralysis of the right hand"), and above all about his artistic work. He continued to draw (notably the impressive *Deluges* now in the Royal Library, Windsor Castle), and to teach (Francesco Melzi,* upon whose work he comments).

What precisely Leonardo was painting while he was in France* is not completely clear. De Beatis specifically mentions seeing three paintings in the workshop.* These have traditionally been thought to be the *Mona Lisa,** *Saint John the Baptist,** and *Virgin and Child with Saint Anne and a Lamb,** but may have been other works now lost. Vasari also mentions a *Saint Anne* cartoon that Francis I wished to see Leonardo "color," and Lomazzo* discusses a *Laughing Pomona,* also painted for the king. These factors present evidence for the argument that Leonardo was more interested in creating new works during the final French period than continuing to work on paintings he had begun in Italy.

Leonardo died in the Clos-Lucé chateau in Amboise, France on May 2, 1519. The French king may have been present. According to Benvenuto Cellini, Francis I "had fallen in love with Leonardo's great virtues and took such great pleasure in hearing him converse

Jean-August Dominique Ingres, *The Death of Leonardo da Vinci,* c. 1818. Pen, brown ink and wash, and graphite. Musée du Louvre, Graphic arts department, Paris.

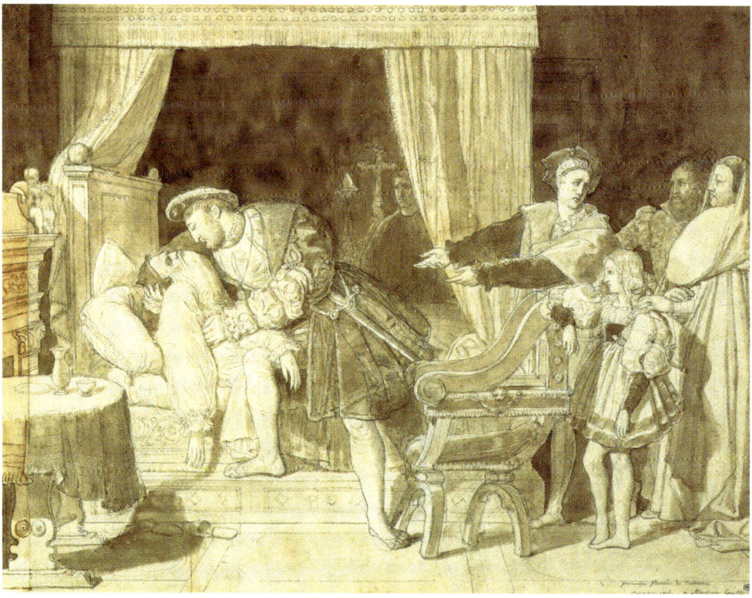

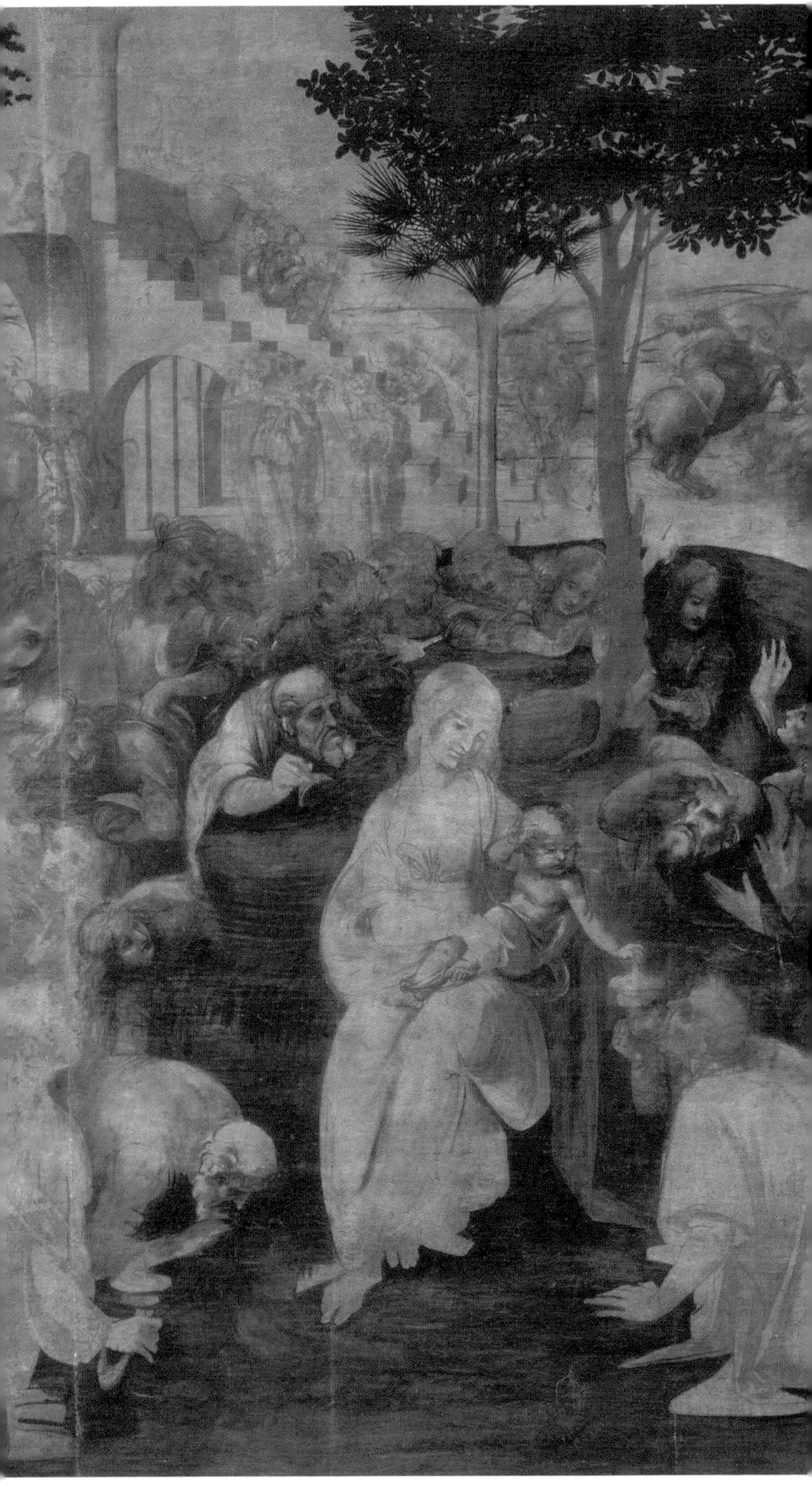

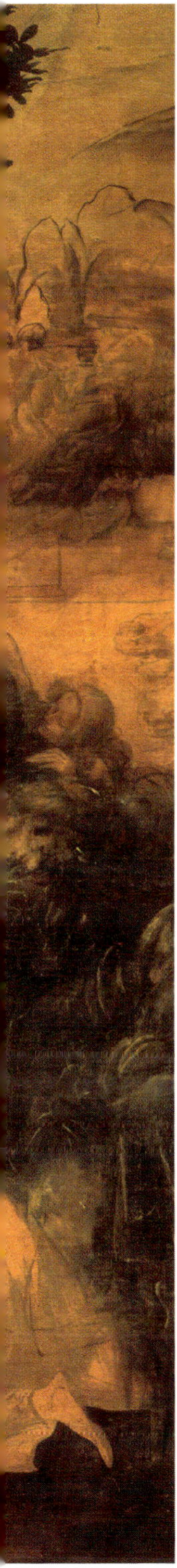

Adoration of the Magi

The *Adoration of the Magi* was commissioned by the brotherhood of the San Donato monastery in Scopeto and is currently in the Galleria degli Uffizi, Florence.

Attribution of this work has never been the source of significant debate. Although it remained uncompleted when Leonardo left Florence* for Milan* in 1482, the painting is still considered the high point of his early period.

The *Adoration* takes up and develops a canonical scene often featured in Quattrocento Florentine art. The originality of Leonardo's treatment lies in the dramatic tension resulting from the complex and dynamic whirl of action and gesture he creates around the Virgin and Child.

Mary and the two figures on each side of her in the foreground are the only stationary figures in the image. Leonardo achieved this effect after a long series of preparatory drawings where he progressively worked out the general compositional structure of the painting and then the details of each figure and their physical position, gesture, and expression. The figures show that he had assimilated and reinterpreted the paintings and sculptures of his contemporaries as well as the repertory of ancient statuary and its use of light and shadow to bring out or de-emphasize volume.

The final image presents a tremendous range of color nuances in almost imperceptible variations of tone. The fine brushwork in yellows, rose brown, and black reveals exceptional mastery in bringing forth forms from the shadows. glazing and varnish—like the colored patina of a bas-relief—blend over earlier sketch work, pentimento, and retouches. Lines of black paint demarcate the contours of the figures arranged in the semicircle closest to Mary.

The background, which was given no over-coating, symbolizes both spatial and temporal distance. It portrays a scene that took place earlier than the one depicted in the foreground—that in which the Magi and their disciples try to construct taller and taller structures from which to view the comet that would lead them to the Messiah.

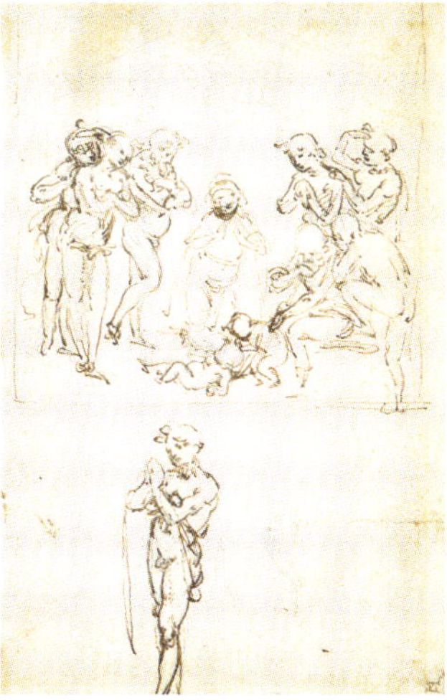

Left: *Adoration of the Magi*, c. 1481–82. Oil on wood panel, 7 ft. 11 7/8 × 8 ft. 1 1/8 in. (243 × 246 cm). Galleria degli Uffizi, Florence.

Above: Study for the *Adoration of the Shepherds*. Pen, brown ink, metal point, prepared paper. Musée Bonnat, Bayonne.

Facing page: Anatomy studies from the *Codex Windsor*, fol. 137 v. Windsor Castle, Royal Library.

Anatomy and Physiognomy

One of Leonardo's essential objectives was to accurately render the human figure. His ambition was to go further than any painter had gone before him in the variety of expressions and evocation of emotions that he was capable of producing. His lifelong studies of anatomy and physiognomy were essential in achieving that goal.

The first step consisted of methodically practicing dissections to attain more than the knowledge offered through books; to go beyond the topographic studies that satisfied most artists of his time. For Leonardo such works were merely preparation for the real study of the functioning of every muscle and organ. He analyzed each body part separately, then put them together to study the whole—sometimes substituting animal organs when human ones were unavailable. He was also interested in the range of bodily and facial positions and expressions, and assembled a collection in his manuscripts,* which he drew upon when needed for a particular subject. As he noted: "The most important thing one can discover in reflecting upon painting are the movements corresponding to the states of mind of every living creature." (*Codex Urbinas* 39 v.) The innumerable drawings that cover the pages of his manuscripts* are much more than simple caricatures drawn in distraction. They are part of the same intense effort to create a visual translation of the most visceral emotions. The richness and variety of expressions found in his oeuvre are the result of this difficult endeavor to understand physiognomy and they correspond to Leonardo's insistence on the infinite diversity and nuances of physiological types. However, his scientific research did not inhibit his visual investigations into the importance of clothing, of which the figurative potential is revealed in his splendid studies of draping. Finally, composition, or the rigorous orchestration of figures, was of absolute importance to the painter; just as every organ plays a role in the harmonious functioning of the body, every human figure had to occupy the compositional position that best served the overall balance in his paintings.

Anatomy studies from the *Codex Windsor*, fol. 122 r. Windsor Castle, Royal Library.

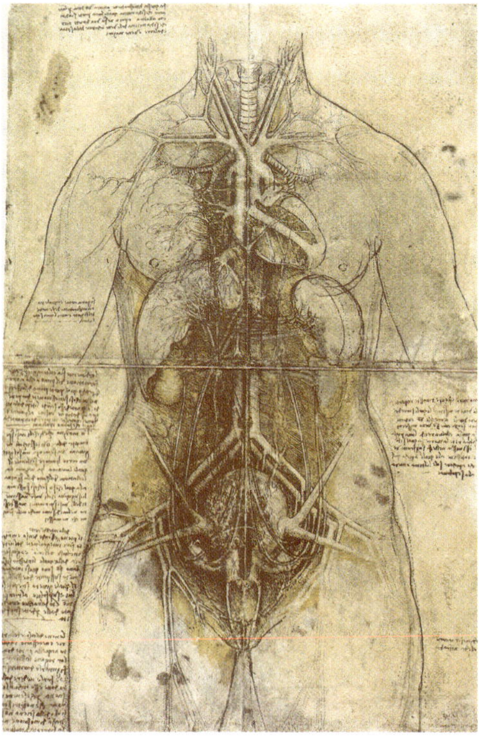

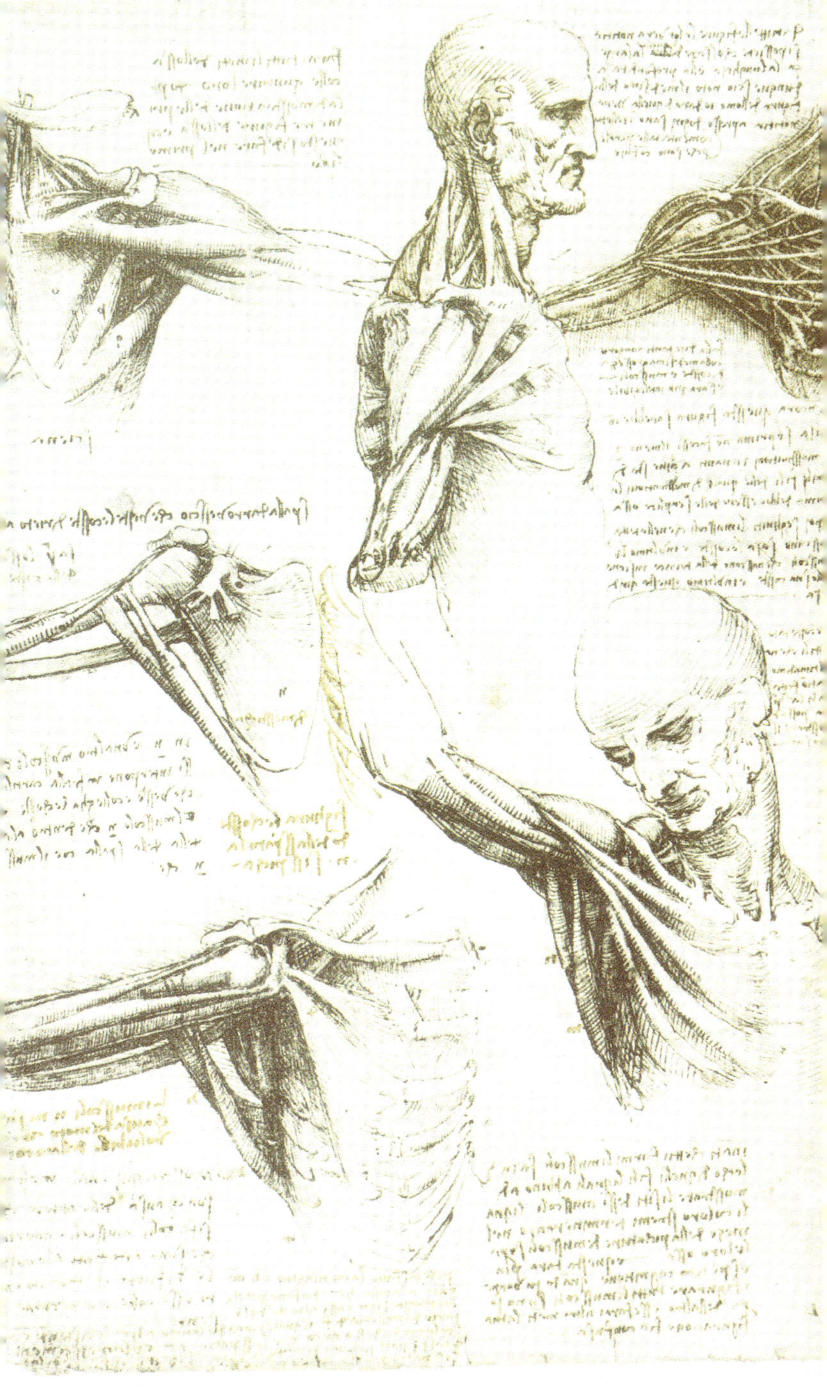

ANNUNCIATION (FLORENCE)

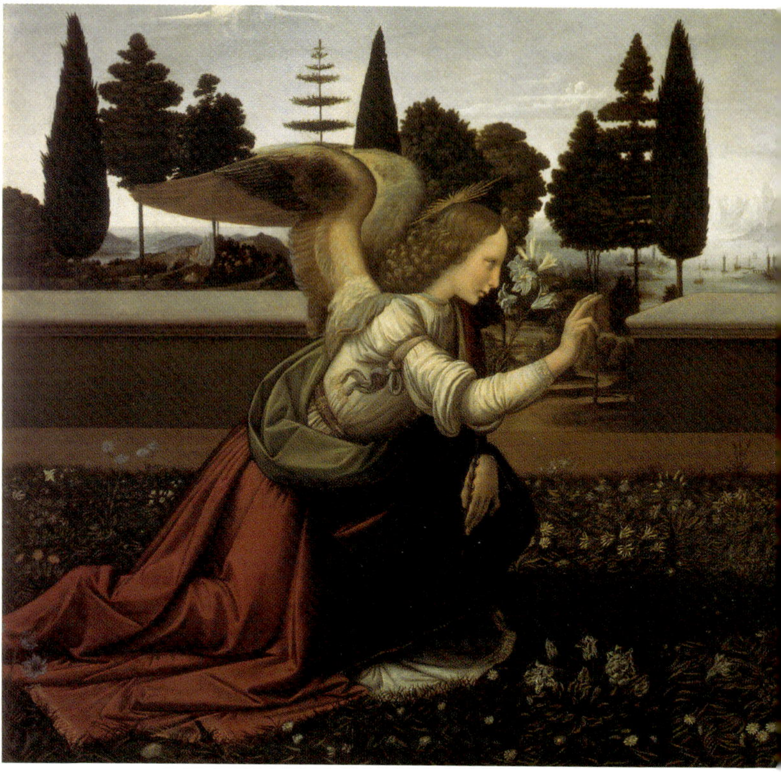

The *Annunciation* in the Galleria degli Uffizi and formerly in the San Bartolomeo church in Monteoliveto was long considered a work of Ghirlandaio. It is now attributed to Leonardo by most art historians who date it 1472–75. For the first time the artist employs techniques, which he had applied and refined on smaller paintings, on a large format. X-rays reveal the great number of changes made to the painting in the course of its execution—indications of the difficulties Leonardo encountered in the construction of space and anatomical* depiction. Several details also point to the influence of Verrocchio's* teaching. The analytic detail and chiseling of each ornamental motif of the Virgin's lectern clearly refers to the sarcophagus for the tomb of Piero de' Medici (church of San Lorenzo, Florence) sculpted by Leonardo's master around the same time. But Leonardo already shows himself capable of surpassing the models provided by his predecessors. Botticelli's typology is taken up and transcended in both Mary's and the angel's faces. The Virgin's right hand and the garlands on the pedestal reveal the painter's fingerprints. Leonardo had already had recourse to such final direct manipulation in the portrait of *Ginevra Benci**—a painterly practice that ran counter to the Florentine conception that painting was

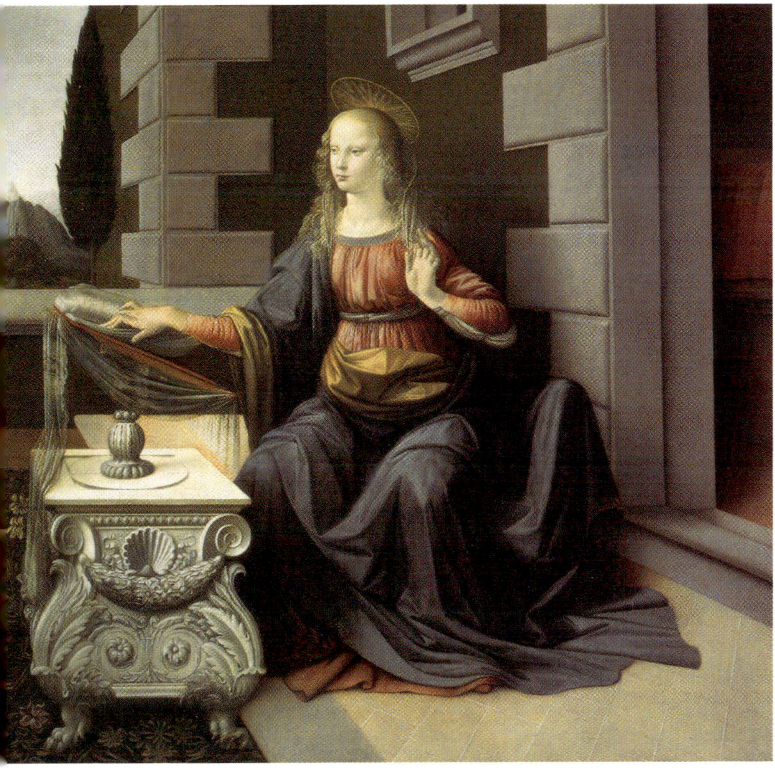

founded on drawing.* The vanishing points meet at the peaks of the snowy mountains that cut into the pale blue sky in the rich landscape of the background (where the boats and the river port reveal a human presence rarely seen in Leonardo's representations of nature). The composition is ordered around the curtain of dark trees, the stone parapet, and the exterior walls of a Tuscan villa recalling the work of Michelangelo. This frame's simplicity brings out the intensity of the dialogue between the protagonists. In this version of a scene often portrayed by Italian painters of the fifteenth century, Leonardo achieves a perfect balance between the portrayal of a spiritual meeting—as Neoplatonic* as it is Christian—and the optical precision of a description of the physical world. His taking up of contemporary Florentine architectural* and sculptural* motifs—which themselves refer, in conformity with humanist precepts, to the art of antiquity—goes exceedingly well with the impassioned depiction of the slightest details, such as the carpet of grass and flowers in the foreground and the sumptuous crisply billowing draping of the clothing.

Annunciation, c. 1472–75. Oil and tempera on wood panel, 3 ft. 2 ½ x 4 ft. 2 in. (98 x 127 cm). Galleria degli Uffizi, Florence.

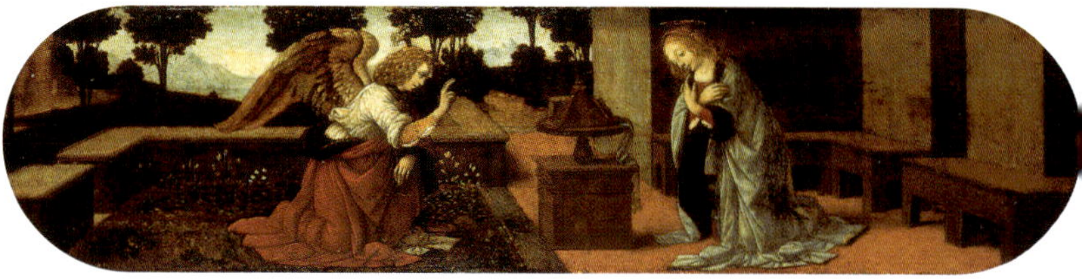

Annunciation. Tempera on wood panel, 6 ⅓ × 23 ⅔ in. (16 × 60 cm). Musée du Louvre, Paris.

Below: Design for a centrally planned church, *Codex B,* c. 1487–90. Bibliothèque de l'Institut de France, Paris.

Annunciation (Louvre)

The small *Annunciation* in the Louvre may be one of the predella panels for an altarpiece Verrocchio* was commissioned to paint for the cathedral of Pistoia, but which is almost entirely the work of Lorenzo di Credi. Despite its weak points, the quality of the faces and the draping has led a number of critics to see at least partial involvement by Leonardo. They refer to similarities in studies in Leonardo's manuscripts* (Galleria degli Uffizi, Florence, inv. 428 Er). Along with the sophisticated Verrocchian elegance and detailed metal work, Leonardian elements include the heads bowed in deep thought, light effects to model volume, and vibrant chiaroscuro. Despite its small size, the composition is quite complex. The articulation created by the stone parapet (to the left) is taken up again and echoed by the stone benches behind the Virgin. Yet the figures fit harmoniously within this rigorous structure. The details in the rendering of Mary express a type of feminine beauty particularly dear to Leonardo. Her clothing is described with an exquisite chromatic range of

ARCHITECTURE

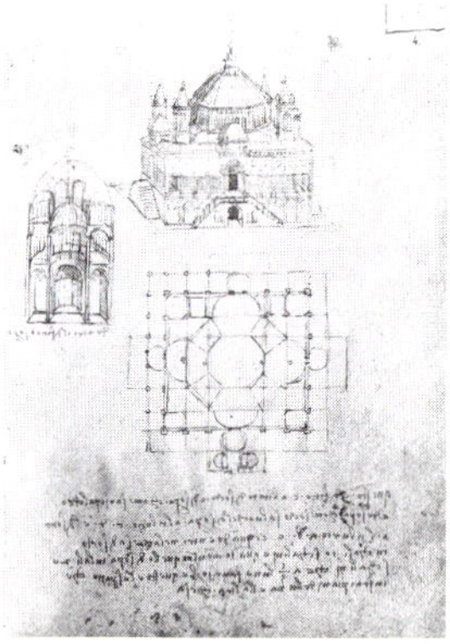

Leonardo had much less of an influence* on architecture than Michelangelo and Raphael. This is evidently because, unlike his two contemporaries, he never succeeded in having his projects built. Nevertheless, manuscripts* and letters indicate not only the importance he placed in his architectural research and designs but also that he personally thought he had attained the same level of excellence in this domain as he had in others. As one would expect, Leonardo delved into architectural theory* as much as he considered its practical aspects. He worked on all sorts of plans, from the renovation of existing buildings and construction of military edifices to more theoretical projects. Like other Quattrocento artists, he put his great mind to designing ideal cities—particularly during his stays in Milan.* Taking up some of the preoccupations of Francesco di Giorgio Martini (Leonardo possessed one of his manuscripts), the artist conceived of the ideal city as an organic whole in which canals, streets, and buildings work together to produce an environment at once harmonious and able to support economic development. His extremely intricate plans reveal purely architectural aspects supplemented with his knowledge of hydraulics and physical mechanics. The Codices of the Institut de France* contain numerous projects for religious architecture with both central plans and layouts in the form of the Latin cross. When in the service of Cesare Borgia, between 1502 and 1503, the fortifications and military engineering projects that Leonardo elaborated were as sophisticated as they were potentially deadly.

blue shades that resonate with the very deep blue of her dress and the lighter blue of her cloak. Gabriel's clothing also reveals the fruit of subtle research on material and color, particularly in his forearm's velvet sleeve and the delicate vermilion draping. The painting's great originality resides in Leonardo's treatment of the background landscape. His setting off of the small trees in the fog differs greatly from conventional gardens seen in work of the period. The tonalities of the pale blue sky also rhyme with the colors of Mary's cloak, while behind the trees the mountain peaks fade off into haze and clouds.

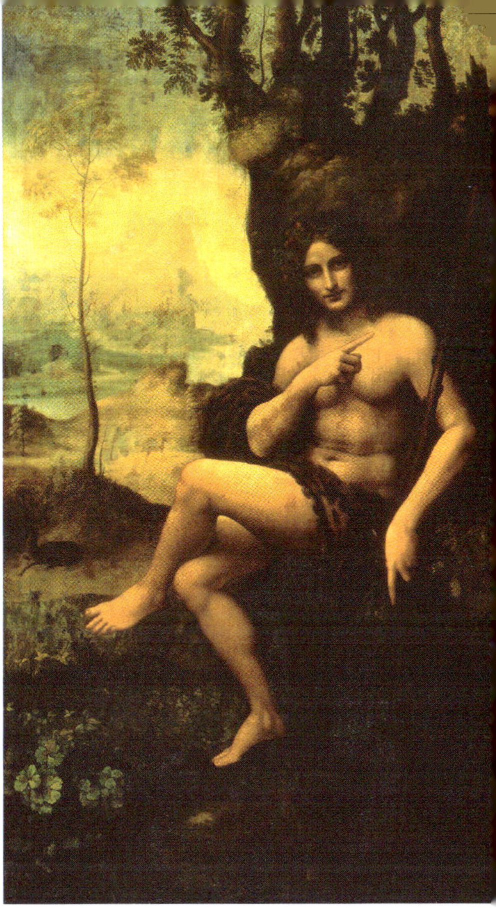

Bacchus or *Saint John the Baptist Seated in the Wilderness*, c. 1510–15. Tempera and oil on canvas (originally on panel), 3 ft. 10 × 3 ft. 9 ¼ in. (117 × 115 cm). Musée du Louvre, Paris.

Bacchus/Saint John the Baptist

When Leonardo died his student Salaì inherited, among other things, a painting now known both as *Saint John the Baptist Seated in the Wilderness* and *Bacchus* (Musée du Louvre, Paris). It was sold in 1525, and a century later Cassiano del Pozzo described it as "Saint John in the Desert" when he saw it at Fontainbleu. In 1695 it was listed in the French royal collection as "Bacchus in a Landscape." In its current state, other than the panther skin, the painting is devoid of Bacchus' traditional attributes (crown of vine leaves, grape cluster, thyrsus). But this is not the case for several early copies. The difficult question is whether the copy painters added the attributes or if they were present in Leonardo's original. Experts are in fact divided on whether the Louvre painting is really a Leonardo autograph. The most probable explanation is that the painting was repainted and modified after the artist's death. Most authorities date it to 1510–15. This work is the subject of countless psychological and psychoanalytic interpretations, most of which are founded upon more or less sexual readings of the young man's state of undress. There are also numerous studies on the originality of the iconography, particularly the way the viewer comes to occupy the position of direct recipient of the saint's message, which contrasts with the composition of most Quattrocento paintings. The combination of these two aspects, plus continued discussion concerning the figure's identity, have led to its being nicknamed "the avenging angel." On top of this, the painting's sad deterioration, and the considerable amount of over-painting it has been subject to, render judgment practically impossible.

ART AND SCIENCE

The essentially close connection between scientific knowledge and the art of painting was at the core of Leonardo's thought. For him, nature could not be represented in its visible manifestations without an understanding of its hidden causes. Remarks in his manuscripts* alternate between the conviction that one must keep close to the appearances of things and a pressing urge to get beyond sensible phenomena to the laws that govern them. To this was added the consistent demand for faithfulness of a concrete representation to correspond to the abstract rules of mathematics. In other words, the artist must be nature's mirror, but the mirror must be conscious—this was the only way of getting beyond commonplace naturalism and arbitrary choices. In his notebooks, Leonardo took on the task of enumerating the infinite components of the visual world in lists as well as a series of drawings.* In this way his work resembles that of writers from his time, such as Politian and Ariosto. But he never stopped at mere juxtaposition, choosing instead a rationally ordered classification, if only that of opposites. For example, he contrasted the delightful with the hideous and sweetness with horror. The four elements and the play of their respective properties, provided another ordering principle he sometimes called upon. But the most subtle of Leonardo's unifying concepts derived from his perception and depiction of hidden analogies among what seemed to be the most disparate natural objects, such as roiling waters and tangled curly tresses (see *Saint John the Baptist*).

Anatomical studies, *Codex Windsor*, fol. 177 r. Windsor Castle, Royal Library.

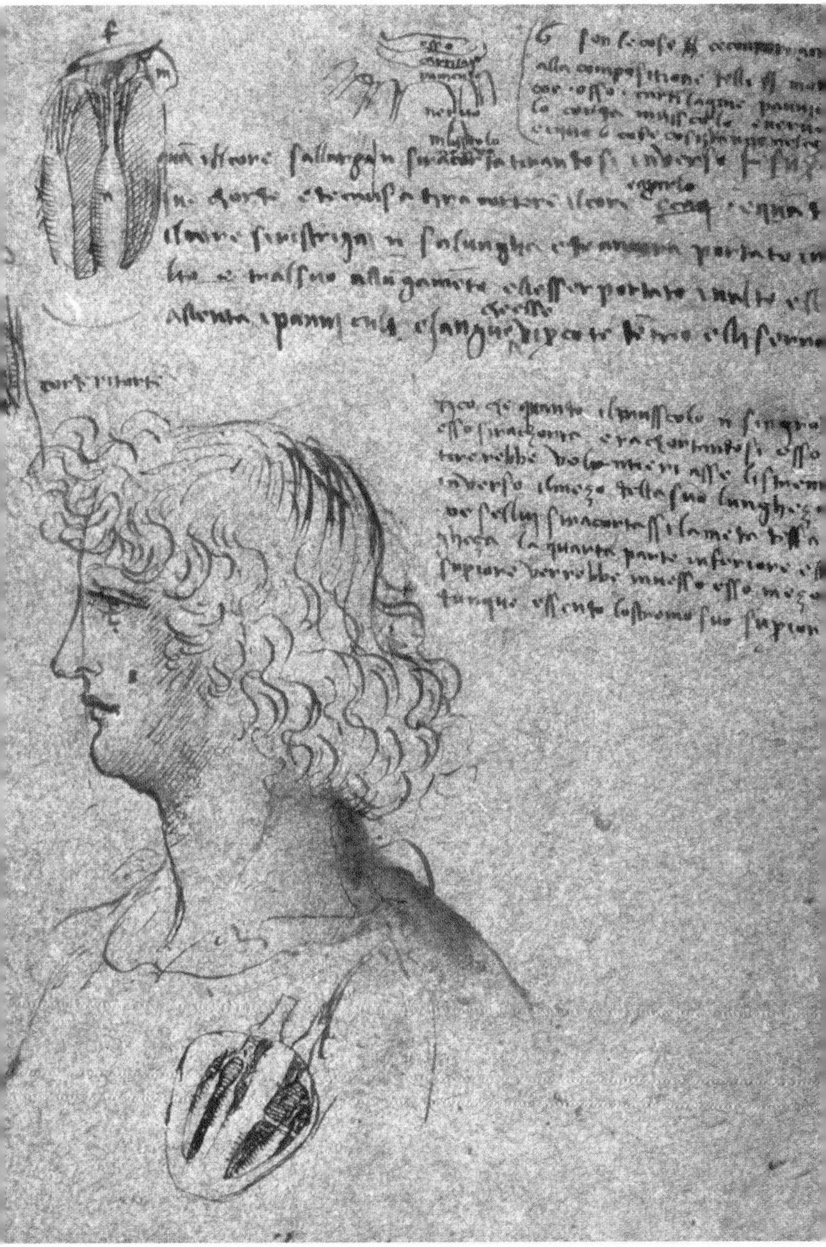

The acquisition of any knowledge is always of use to the intellect, because it may thus drive out useless things and retain the good. For nothing can be loved or hated unless it is first known.

(*Codex Atlanticus,* 226 v., Richter, 1172)

Baptism of Christ

Representative of the complex relations between Leonardo and Verrocchio,* the *Baptism of Christ* (Galleria degli Uffizi, Florence) was long considered an early Leonardo work. According to Vasari,* Leonardo stepped in to work on the picture already started by his master, painting the angel in the left foreground, reworking the background at left, and revising Christ's body. These elements clearly differ from the rest of the painting. The stiff figure of John the Baptist contrasts with that of the angel in profile so delicately modeled by the light, which also reflects off of its wavy blond hair; the stiff, nearly metallic, palm tree seems almost diagrammatic in comparison to the vast landscape opening up behind the two angels. Quattrocento Florentine painting habitually presented valley views punctuated with elegantly stylized cypresses and poplars. Natural elements were only used for measuring off the space behind human figures. Leonardo brought an entirely new view of nature and the human figure, resulting from his serious study of anatomy,* his mastery of the representation of movement, his ability to render the qualities of specific materials by using subtle light effects, and his capacity to translate the range of his protagonists' emotions into paint. The angel he added to his master's painting reconciles two aspects of the representation of the human figure, which until then had been separated, or in any case poorly linked, by Italian paintings: precision of physical description and the convincing expression of a psychological and spiritual situation. The combination of Leonardo's profound assimilation of scientific knowledge (see Art and Science) with the harmony of his pictorial forms brought about an organic vitality that effectively symbolized the unity of mind and matter.

Leonardo da Vinci and Andrea Verrocchio, *Baptism of Christ,* 1475–78. Oil on canvas, 5 ft. 9 ⅝ × 4 ft. 11 ½ in. (180 × 151 cm). Galleria degli Uffizi, Florence.

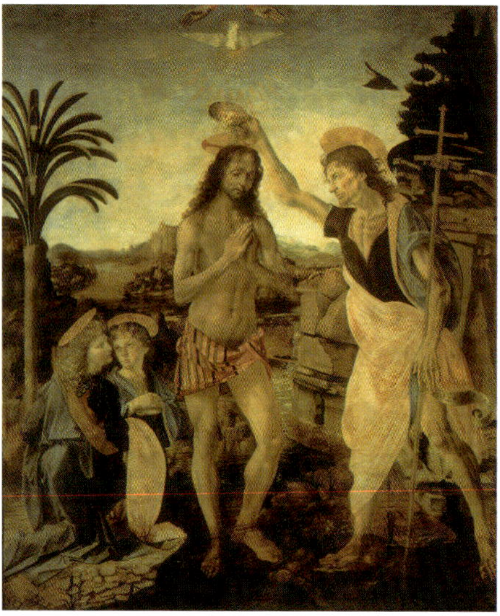

Beauty

Nowhere in his written works does Leonardo venture to elaborate, even summarily, a definition of beauty. This is because for him it was the end towards which all painting aspired. Painting was non-conceptual thought, but it included by processes of metaphor, and exceeded by the play of ambiguity, rational and scientific thought. His insistence on the analogy between the microcosm and the macrocosm is well known. For him, this correspondence gradually became the illustration of a more general law by which each form was only the instrument or the trace of a natural power in action. Using analogy, the painter was then at liberty to create imaginary but plausible creatures because they were based on directly observable entities in the real world. "You know that you cannot invent animals without limbs, each of which, in itself, must resemble those of some other animal. Hence if you wish to make an animal, imagined by you, appear natural—let us say a Dragon, take for its head that of a mastiff or hound, with the eyes of a cat, the ears of a porcupine, the nose of a greyhound, the brow of a lion, the temples of an old cock, the neck of a water tortoise." (*Codex A*, Institut de France 109 r., Richter, 585) Still, these considerations became less important for him as he became more and more fascinated with beauty born through ambiguity. The loveliness of a face for example, obtained through the subtle play of shade and light: "The utmost grace [is conferred by] the shadows and lights added to the faces of those who sit in the darkened doorways of their dwellings. Then the eye of the beholder observes the shaded part of the face thrown into deeper shade by the shadows from the aforesaid dwellings, and sees brightness added to the illuminated part of the face by the radiance of the atmosphere. Because of such increases in the shadows and lights the face acquires great relief, and in the illuminated part the shadows are almost indistinguishable, and in the shaded part the lights are almost indistinguishable. The face depicted in this way acquires much beauty with the increase in shadows and lights." (*Codex Urbinas* 41 v., 42 r., Kemp and Walker, 215–16) The suppression of color and the elimination of precision in drawing, which occur more and more frequently in the later work, are the price to pay for beauty that challenges obvious splendor in favor of enigmatic charm. Such an attitude then opens the way for an aesthetic of the incomplete along with its beautiful unexpected effects and developments.

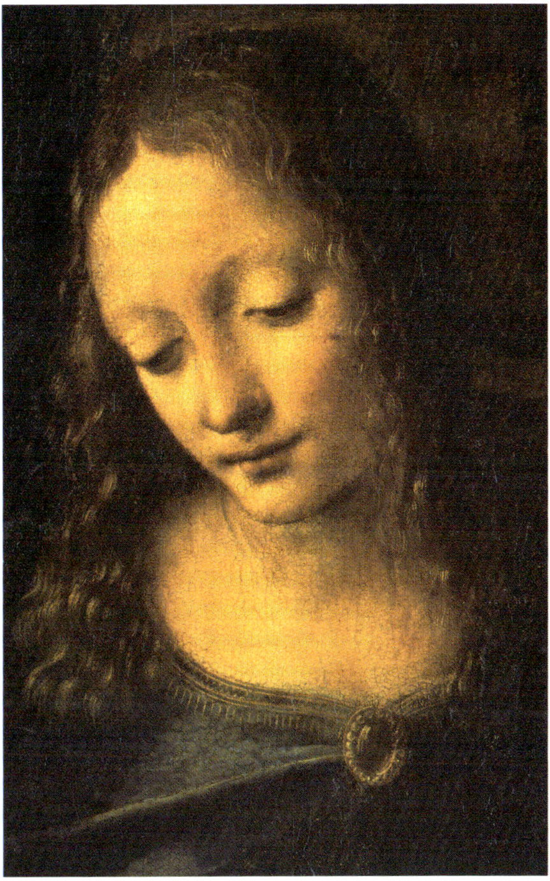

Virgin of the Rocks (detail), c. 1483–86. Oil on wood panel. Musée du Louvre, Paris.

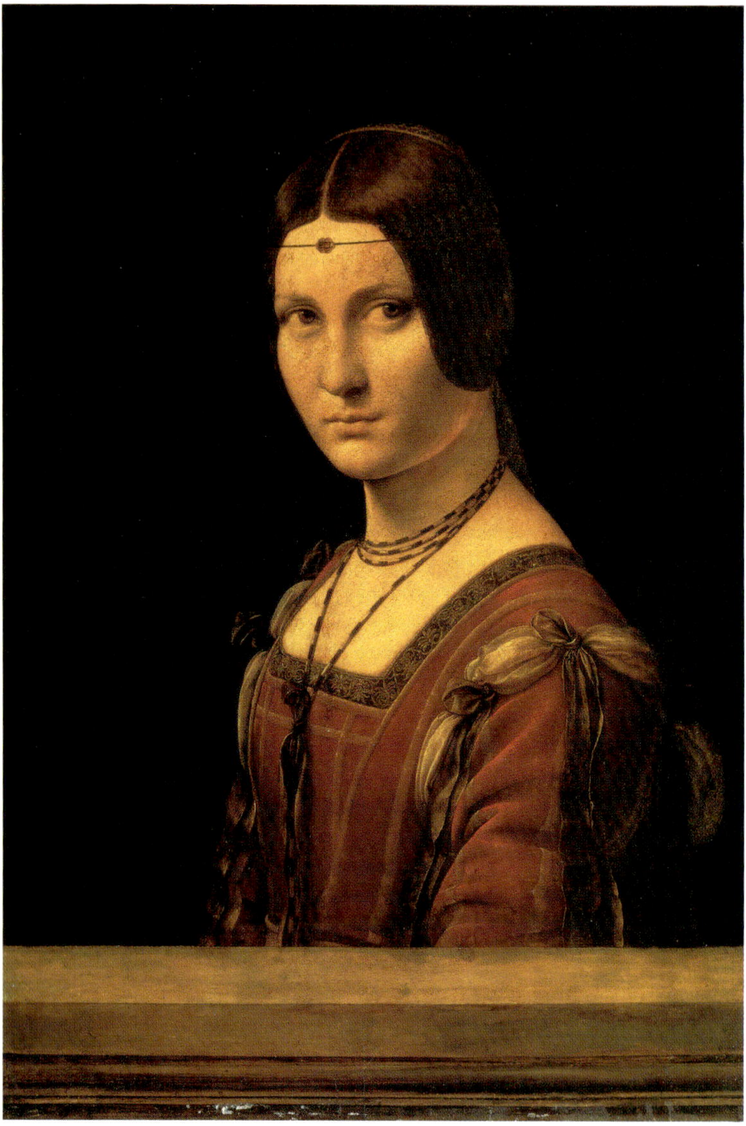

Appetite is the support of life.
Fear or timidity is the prolongation of life
and preservation of its instruments.

(*Codex Atlanticus,* 170 r., Richter, 842)

BELLE FERRONNIÈRE

The *Belle Ferronière*, also known as *Portrait of a Woman of the Court of Milan* and *Portrait of a Lady* (Musée du Louvre, Paris) was probably painted between 1490 and 1495. It is the last portrait made by Leonardo during his first period in Milan* and the technique closely resembles that of *The Musician** and *Lady with an Ermine.** While it is now generally accepted as a work of the master, its attribution to Leonardo had long been contested (parts or the whole were attributed to Boltraffio*). The identity of the subject, however, has never been established, but the most reasonable hypothesis, given what we know today, is that the sitter was Lucrezia Crivelli, a mistress of Ludovico Sforza. The composition reveals the influence of Antonello de Messina: the bust-length model is placed behind a parapet and set against a dark ground to produce an effective sense of depth. But as Peitro Marani has noted, Leonardo created an extremely subtle way of accentuating the sculptural volumes sought by his predecessor. The impossibility of meeting the gaze of the beautiful young woman forces the viewer to continually change position before her as if one were attempting to walk around a sculpture. Here we find one of several examples of Leonardo's transposition of principles he was developing for the equestrian monument to Francesco Sforza (see Sculpture) onto a two-dimensional surface. This painting also indicates his mastery of subtle tonal gradations. Note the vibrating shadow and light of his chiaroscuro in the reflection of rose-colored light on the curve of the left cheek, resulting from the refraction of light from the shoulder and the red velvet dress onto the jaw. The painting is the successful expression of Leonardo's study of colored, synthesized shadows as described in the *Treatise on Painting**: "reflections of skin on other skin are more rose colored and of a better complexion than any other." The unusual roundness of the face had to have been conceived in order to better explore the difficult question of colored light reflected on a spherical body in partial darkness. With this said, it must be added that so much physico-mathematical virtuosity would only have produced gratuitous effects had it not been put to the service of a most acute psychological analysis.

Belle Ferronière, c. 1490–95. Oil on wood panel, 24 ½ x 17 ⅜ in. (62 x 44 cm). Musée du Louvre, Paris.

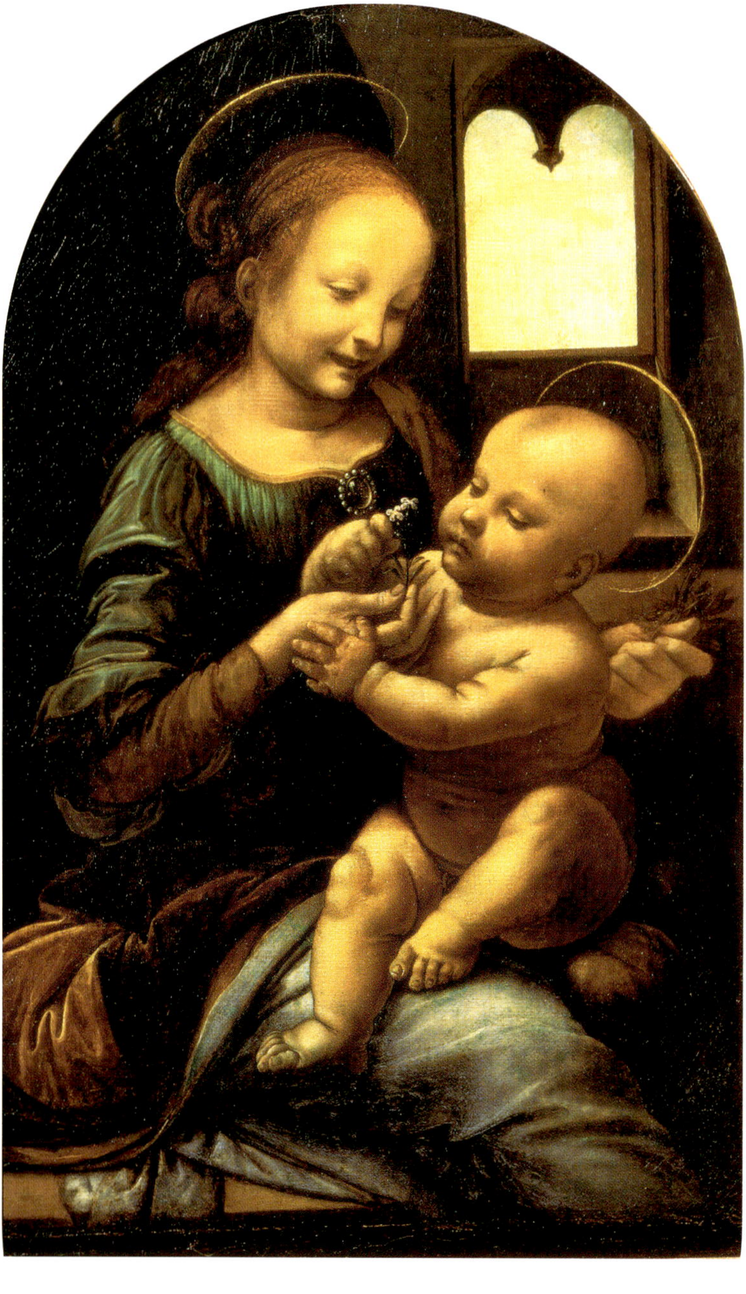

The natural desire of good men is knowledge.

(*Codex Atlanticus*, 119 v., McCurdy, 53)

BENOIS MADONNA

This Virgin and Child is called the *Benois Madonna* (Hermitage Museum, Saint Petersburg) after the family that owned it until the beginning of the nineteenth century. It is possibly one of "two Virgin Marys" Vasari* describes Leonardo as having started in 1478 and on which he was still working when he left for Milan* in 1482. It was not until the beginning of the twentieth century that it became accessible to specialists after appearing in a group exhibition with other works from private Russian collections. Nothing is known of its history. Originally painted on a wood panel, it was transferred onto canvas when Czar Nicholas II acquired it in 1914. Laboratory analyses show that a landscape had appeared through the window but was painted over. This suggests that the painting may not have been finished. Still, a Leonardo who had left most of his early compositional techniques behind him and almost entirely freed himself of Verrocchio's* influence is evident. The Virgin's lively, animated and smiling expression seems to bear out Leonardo's interest in Desiderio da Settignano's sculptures. This is the first time the painter has used the form of an upside-down isosceles triangle in the rendering of a protagonist's face, an approach which enabled him to give the character grace and balance while maintaining conformity to the real shape of the human face. The Virgin's head appears more solidly structured and more carefully rendered than the angel's in the *Baptism of Christ.** It also differs greatly from those in the two versions of the *Annunciation,** the *Dreyfus* Madonna,* and the *Madonna of the Carnation.** The *Benois Madonna* is thus a transitional work, prefiguring later expressive typologies such as in the *Adoration of the Magi.** But it is most important due to Leonardo's new technique for modeling figures within an interior space. He carefully balances two distinct light sources, one coming from the window in the back wall and the other flowing down from somewhere in the upper left beyond the picture frame. He later described such modeling of figures in chiaroscuro with strong shadow and light effects (see Beauty, "The utmost grace . . ."). Considering the number of times the work was copied by Florentine painters—there is a fine example by Filippo Lippi in Rome, (Galleria Colonna)—the extent of its success is not difficult to measure.

Benois Madonna, c. 1478–82.
Oil on wood panel transferred to canvas,
19 ½ x 12 ⅓ in. (49.5 x 31.5 cm).
Hermitage Museum, Saint Petersburg.

Boltraffio, Giovanni Antonio

Giovanni Antonio Boltraffio (1467–1516) came from a comfortable bourgeois family in Milan* and was probably Leonardo's student during the early 1490s; Leonardo's notebooks of c. 1491, in fact, mention a "Gian Antonio." In any event, lessons learned from Leonardo are evident in Boltraffio's earliest works, where they are interpreted in a very personal way, as in the *Resurrection with Saints Leonard and Lucy* (Staatliche Museen, Berlin), executed in collaboration with Marco d'Oggiono. The influence* of the Tuscan master is combined with those of Perugino, Bolognese masters (particularly Francesco Francia), and Lombard painters such as Ambrogio Bergognone, Bramantino, and Solario.*

The scope and variety of Boltraffio's explorations during this period make establishing a catalog of his early work difficult. Attribution of a number of works is still debated by specialists. Some are attributed to other members of the workshop* or other Milanese artists. Boltraffio was active at the court of Ludovico Sforza, where his portraits were especially appreciated, and he soon had an eminent reputation. In 1498 Isabella of Aragon, the widow of Gian Galeazzo Sforza, sent him to Mantua to copy a portrait of her brother Ferrante. He was probably in Bologna in 1500 painting the Santa Maria della Misericordia altarpiece for the poet Gerolamo Casio for whom he had painted a fine portrait several years earlier (Pinacoteca di Brera, Milan). Back in Milan he painted a *Saint Barbara* (Staatliche Museen, Berlin) for the congregation of the Santa Maria presso Saint Satiro. The next year he was a member of the commission judging models for one of the cathedral doors. It is possible that he was in Rome* in 1506, as the fresco representing the *Virgin and Child with the Donor Francesco Cabañas* (Sant'Onofrio, Rome) seems to bear the mark of his brush, but its authorship is still being debated. In 1508 he painted an altarpiece (Szépmüsvézeti Muzeum, Budapest) for the Bassano da Ponte family chapel in the Lodi Cathedral. Later works include a *Bust of Christ* in the Crespi collection, Milan; a presumed portrait of Costanza Bentivoglio, (Chatsworth); a *Young Man with an Arrow* in the Lord Elgin Collection, Scotland; a *Portrait of a Woman* held in the Galleria Borghese, Rome; as well as several *Madonnas* such as the one in the Museo Poldi Pezzoli, Milan.

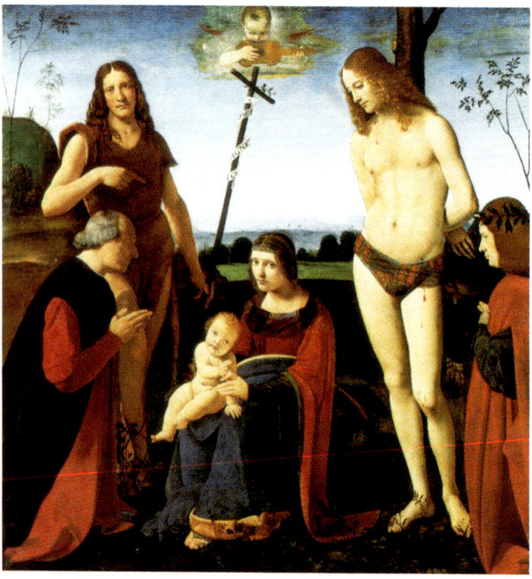

Giovanni Antonio Boltraffio, *Virgin and Child with Saints John the Baptist and Sebastian and Two Donors,* c. 1500. Oil on canvas. Musée du Louvre, Paris.

Bramante, Donato

The architect Donato Bramante (1444–1514) began his artistic education in Urbino, where he was an enthusiast of the complex mathematical games then in vogue at the court of Montefeltro. After 1477 he was in Lombardy, where he continued his architectural experiments which culminated in the impressive church of Santa Maria presso San Satiro in Milan. Its construction began in 1482, that is to say the very year Leonardo arrived in Milan.* Unlike the work of Tuscan architects, Bramante used perspective less as a rational instrument of measure, than as a visual tool for producing illusionist effects. The same can be said of his pictorial production during his time in Milan, in particular in the frescoes of armed men he did for the Casa Oanigarola-Prinetti (Pinacoteca di Brera, Milan). He abandoned more facile trompe l'oeil effects for the rigorously balanced Santa Maria delle Grazie, built with a unified structure on a central plan between 1492 and 1497. Upon being called to Rome* by Pope Julius II, in 1500, he dedicated himself to the search for perfectly harmonious proportions and then applied his latest theories in his plans for the monastery of Santa Maria della Pace (1500–04). Above all, it was at this time that he saw for himself the actual Roman ruins that he had previously known only through theoretical treatises and engravings. In his project for the new Saint Peter's Basilica commissioned by Julius II, he conceived of a series of enormous volumes, on the model of Roman architecture, which fit inside each other spectacularly to occupy the maximum amount of space possible. Julius rejected the plan, judging it impossible to build. Bramante found the opportunity to apply his perfectly harmonious proportions on a smaller scale in the Tempietto on the grounds of the San Pietro monastery in Montorio, where he struck a fine balance between a return to a formal repertory of ancient origin and faithfulness to the Christian sanctity of the structure. His plans for the Belvedere court in the Vatican palace indicate a return to a conception of architecture that gave a large place to illusionist and theatrical effects. He died before completing the design.

Donato Bramante, *Tempietto,* c. 1510. San Pietro in Montori, Rome.

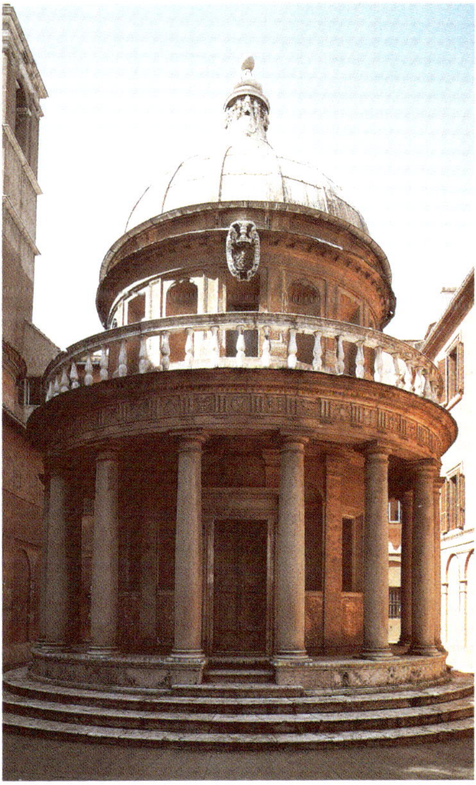

BURLINGTON HOUSE CARTOON

The attribution of *Saint Anne, the Virgin, the Infant Jesus, and Saint John the Baptist*, also known as the *Burlington House Cartoon* (National Gallery, London) is undisputed, even if no signed Leonardo da Vinci painting deriving from it exists. On the other hand, Bernardino Luini* did use it, adding in the figure of Joseph, for his painting of the Holy Family (Pinacoteca Ambrosiana, Milan). Dating it has proved to be less unanimous. Most Italian experts place it between 1501 and 1505, while English and American specialists consider 1506–08 as more likely. If the first hypothesis is correct, it is possible that the work is the result of a commission by King Louis XII after his occupation of Milan* in 1499. In any case, its majestic sculptural dimensions reveal detailed knowledge of ancient sculpture* (particularly the *Muses* formerly in the Villa Adriana in Tivoli, now in the Prado) he would have acquired when he was in Rome.* This is undeniably one of Leonardo's most classically inspired works, which may explain why he eventually abandoned it, since it is rare to find, among his paintings, a scene of such serenity and balance without the play of forces of nature and without oppositions between contrasting movements. The pyramidal composition, which would inspire Raphael in the *Madonnas* of his Florentine period, the fluidity of the draping, and the elegant composure of the postures all add to this impression. The grouping of figures is like that of the *Virgin of the Rocks** but modified by greater naturalism. It is conceived as a unitary and stable block with each protagonist seemingly experiencing a particular nuanced emotion, while always being tinged with sadness, and in the end ambiguity—a fact that has led to considerable interpretative debates. In any event, one cannot help but be struck by the contrast between the almost sleepy innocence of the Virgin's expression and the irony of Anne's, emphasized in the curl of her lips and the depth of her gaze. Some commentators have seen this as a veiled warning or cryptic allusion to Christ's Passion. As his manuscripts* attest, Leonardo's incessant exploration of emotion, thought, and their exterior manifestations, including the most elusive, come together as a sort of meditation on the human condition and its relation to the divine.

Saint Anne, the Virgin, the Infant Jesus, and Saint John the Baptist, (*Burlington House Cartoon*), 1498–1500. Charcoal, black and white chalk on tinted paper, 4 ft. 6 ¾ x 3 ft. 3 ⅞ in. (141.5 x 104.6 cm). National Gallery, London.

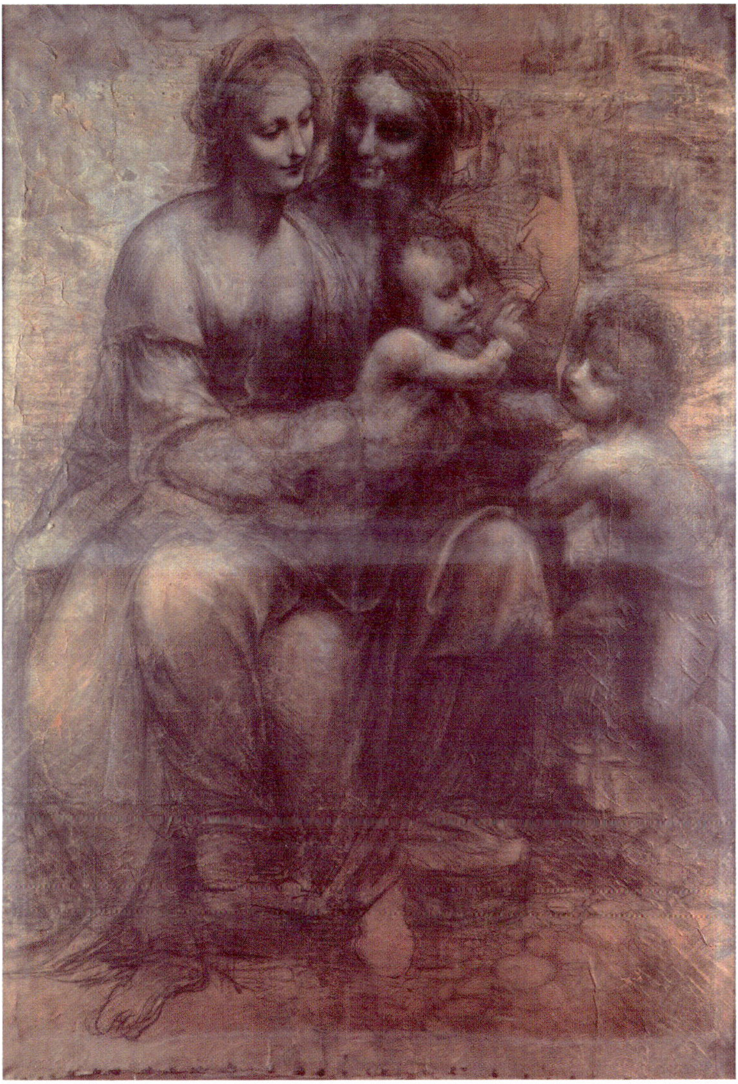

Just as iron rusts unless it is used,
and water purifies or, in cold, turns to ice,
so our intellect spoils unless it is kept in use.

(*Codex Atlanticus,* 289 v.c., Richter, 1177)

Cesare da Sesto

Little is known of the early life and work of Cesare da Sesto (c. 1477–1523), but most art historians agree that he probably received his first artistic apprenticeship in Milan* where he discovered the great influence* of his career—Leonardo's paintings. The earliest references to him concern work on Julius II's apartments in the Vatican in 1508. Such a prestigious commission suggests that he had already achieved some notoriety by that point. He also collaborated with Baldassare Peruzzi on the monastery of Sant'Onofrio in Rome,* where he painted a *Virgin and Child with a Donor*. In addition, there is a *Virgin and Child with Saint John the Baptist* (Campagnano Romano, parish church) dating from the same period. Its subject matter, as much as its style, is clearly inspired by Leonardo's prototypes. Back in Milan in 1510, among other works, Cesare painted an appealing *Baptism of Christ* (Gallarati Scotti Collection, Milan). He then traveled to the center and south of the Italian peninsula. In Messina he painted an altarpiece, *Virgin and Child with Saint John the Baptist and Saint George* (M. H. De Young Memorial Museum, San Francisco) for the San Giorgio dei Genoese confraternity and an *Adoration of the Magi* (Museo di Capodimonte, Naples), which greatly influenced painters there. For the San Domenico monastery in Catania, he painted an altarpiece, most of which was destroyed in the seventeenth century; only a fragment with Mary's face survives (*in situ*). His activity in central Italy is less well known, and most specialists remain unconvinced about efforts at attributing paintings there to him. Cesare probably returned to Milan in 1520. The only evidence relating to his later life is a contract dated January 23, 1523 for the painting, within six months, of a large polyptych altarpiece for the church of San Rocco (Castello Sforzesco, Milan); the artist died before it was completed.

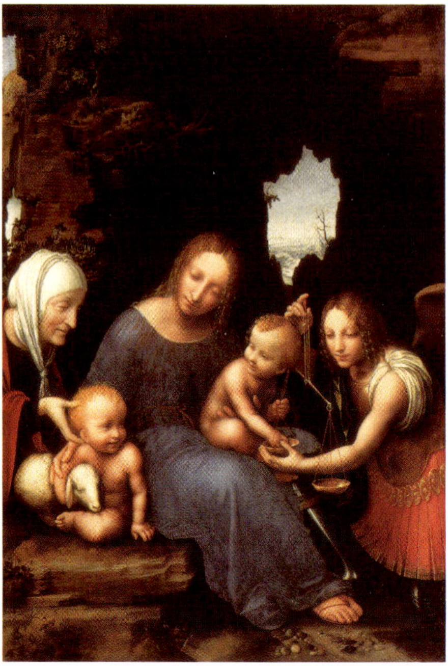

Cesare da Sesto, *Virgin with Scales*. Oil on canvas, 3 ft. 1 ½ × 2 ft. 1 in. (95 × 69 cm). Musée du Louvre, Paris.

Codex Arundel

The *Codex Arundel* (British Museum, London) is named for its first owner, Thomas Howard, Earl of Arundel. He probably acquired it, in Spain, in the 1630s. Unlike most Leonardo manuscripts,* it is not comprised of separate sheets, but is bound together in volumes that largely maintain Leonardo's original order. The *Codex Arundel* is mainly devoted to mathematical topics, but also touches on physics, optics (see *Sfumato*), astronomy, and architecture.* It contains less stimulating records on expenses and notes, for which the main interest is their usefulness in dating the pages. Comentators have been struck by the coolness with which Leonardo makes note of his father's death: "On the 9th of July 1504, Wednesday, at seven o'clock, died Ser Piero da Vinci, notary at the Palazzo del Podesta, my father,—at seven o'clock, being eighty years old, leaving behind ten sons and two daughters." (Richter, 1372) A significant number of pages concern the project for Francis I's new Romorantin residence. It included a vast complex of constructions and gardens on either side of the Sandre River and was to include the fifteenth-century palace of the king's ancestors. But in 1509 an epidemic that was probably caused by the insalubrity of the site led the king to abandon it in favor of Chambord. Finally, the *Codex Arundel* contains some especially significant and original pages, for example the design drawings* for a device with a mask and pipes for breathing under water, or notes and sketches for stage sets for Politian's drama "Orpheus," which was performed in Milan between 1506 and 1508. These included a complex mechanism Leonardo designed so that the actor playing Pluto could appear spectacularly through a hole in the floor, representing a mountain chasm (see Entertainments).

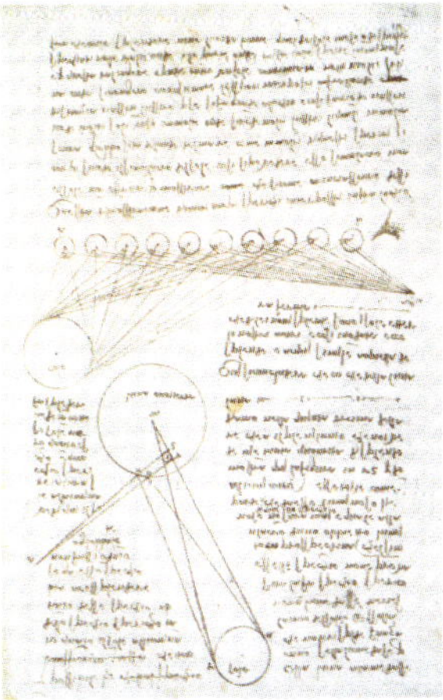

Studies of the sun and moon, *Codex Arundel*, 263, fol. 28 v., c. 1508. British Museum, London.

Codex Atlanticus

The *Codex Atlanticus* (Biblioteca Ambrosiana, Milan) is the largest group of Leonardo's manuscripts* currently preserved. The name derives from the format of its pages, similar in size to those of an atlas. It covers nearly all of Leonardo's career, a forty-year period between 1478 and 1519. Leonardo's studies in mathematics, astronomy, physical geography, botany, and chemistry can be found here. But it also contains projects for war machines, flying machines, submarines, complex mechanical devices, and objects for daily use, as well as several city and architectural plans, which were never realized. These run from his first studies for redeveloping Milan* to the project for a French royal residence in Romorantin, and include plans for a new Medici palace in Florence.* On top of all this, the *Codex Atlanticus* chronicles Leonardo's thinking through a series of Fables,* Humorous* remarks, and philosophical meditations. From a more strictly artistic perspective, the pages contain many important notes on theoretical and practical aspects of sculpture* and painting, perspective, effects of light and shadow, and the materials to be used in the workshop.* All of this elucidation is accompanied by preliminary drawings* for painted or sculpted works—for example the *Adoration of the Magi,* Leda and the Swan,* the *Battle of Anghiari,* and the equestrian monuments that were planned to honor Francesco Sforza and Gian Giacomo Trivulzio. The pages of the *Codex Atlanticus* are thus an irreplaceable document for an overview of Leonardo's art and thinking—no serious study of Leonardo can avoid referring to it.

Codex on the Flight of Birds

Thanks to the Sabachnikoff family, this thirteen-page manuscript* was acquired by the Italian Royal family in 1893. It is still held in the Biblioteca Reale of Turin and is named for it subject matter. Leonardo had devoted much time and unfruitful effort developing theories and mechanisms of artificial flight during his first Milan* period. Upon returning to Florence* in 1500 he turned his attention to detailed analysis of the flight of birds. After five years he had gathered a great many observations on how birds in flight react to wind and air currents. He distinguished two main categories of movement, "one like a spiral or screw, the other rectilinear and curved," but it was the first of these which fascinated him. "This bird flies ever higher by using a circular spiraling motion and will react to the coming of a wind burst and its passing by turning purposefully to its right and left." He understood this as an expression of nature's vital energy also found in the circulation of blood within bodies, the spinning of whirlpools, and the ramifications of branches on plants. He translated this into his paintings from the same period, the serpentine lines of *Leda and the Swan,* or the tangle of overlapping horses in the *Battle of Anghiari.* In 1505 Leonardo began once again to work on his project for a flying machine. This time, adding what he had learned from his observations concerning birds in flight, the

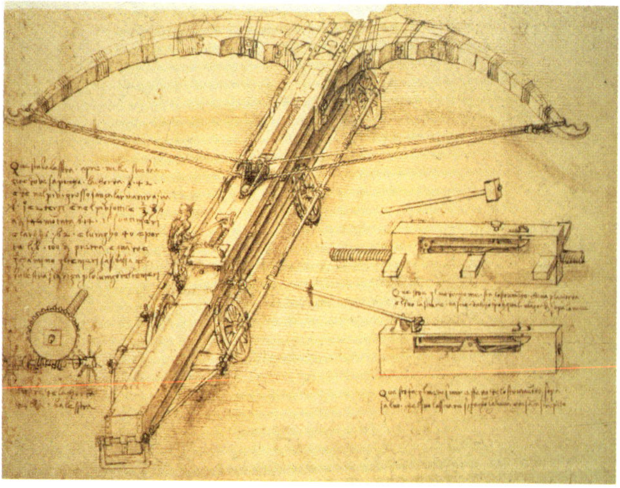

Giant catapult, *Codex Atlanticus,* c. 1499. Biblioteca Ambrosiana, Milan.

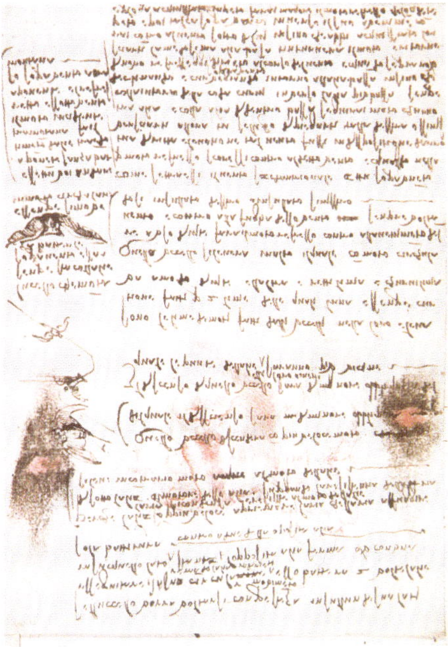

principle of gravity, and the mechanics of weight, he came up with a machine that required little muscular effort on the part of the person powering it. It was designed to make use of air currents and had large moveable wings similar to those of bats. He accompanied his diagrams with a passionate argument against future objections, and this prophesy: "The Great Bird will take off from the summit of the Cecero (a large hill near Florence) providing subject matter for every pen and assuring eternal glory for the nest where it was born."

Codex Forster

Although they are quite different in content, the three Forster notebooks share a common history. After belonging to Pompeo Leoni (see Manuscripts*) they went to Lord Lytton's collection and then to John Forster's before going to the Victoria and Albert Museum in 1876. The *Codex Forster I* is comprised of two manuscripts. The first dates to between 1487 and 1490, and indicates Leonardo's interest in hydrology. It presents several projects for water-powered machines. *Codex Forster I* also contains Leonardo's reflections on "perpetual motion," a subject the author later repudiated as a form of "superstition." The second part of *Codex Forster I*, which dates to 1505, is devoted to stereometry, the geometric study of solid bodies, or as Leonardo put it, "the transformation of one body to another without material reduction or augmentation." Unlike most of Leonardo's manuscripts, it is very well organized and is divided into three sections:

Give your master the instance of a captain who does not himself win the victory, but the soldiers do by his counsels; and so he still deserves the reward.

(*Codex Forster* II, 15 v., Richter, 1400)

Above:
A page from the *Codex on the Flight of Birds.* Pen and ink on paper. Biblioteca Reale, Turin.

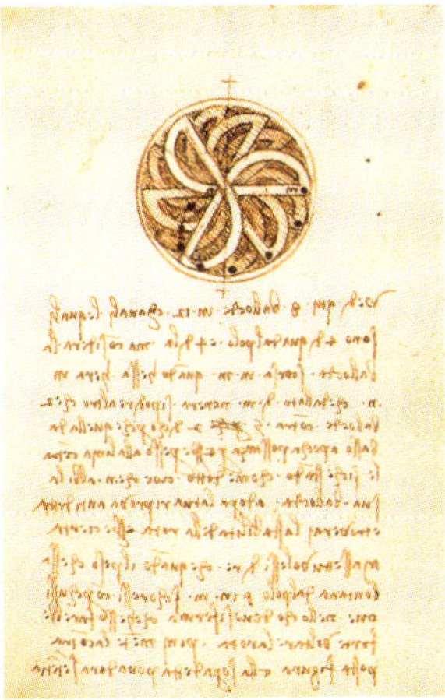

Right:
Codex Forster II, 90 v. Victoria and Albert Museum, London.

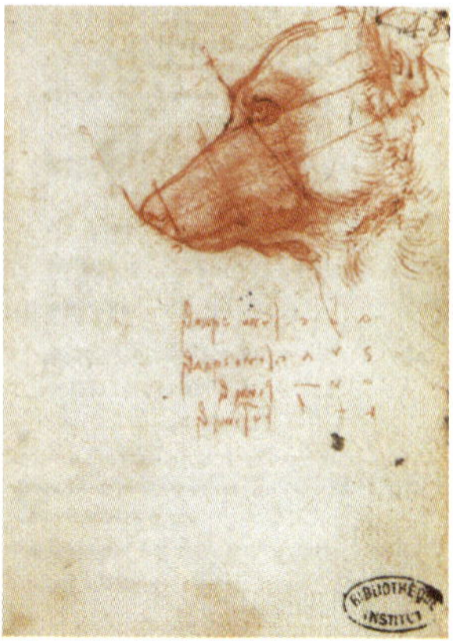

Head of a dog and architectural design, *Codex I*, c. 1497–99. Bibliothèque de l'Institut de France, Paris.

two-dimensional geometry, three-dimensional geometry, and pyramidal transformations. His research in these areas is based on Euclid's theories and the works of the humanist Luca Pacioli. Leonardo illustrated Pacioli's *De divina proportione* with five neoplatonically* derived "regular bodies." *Codex Forster II* is also comprised of two manuscripts. The first (1495) is actually a notebook of exercises in physics, which should be examined in relation to a treatise on the subject that Leonardo mentions having completed, but which is unfortunately lost to us today. The second (c. 1497) is principally made up of drawings* in red chalk, including very fine groupings devoted to Bramante's* architectural works in Milan* and splendid intertwining vegetation later represented on a larger scale in the Sala delle Asse.* *Codex Forster III* is a small book of about one hundred pages dating from 1493 to 1496. It combines the most disparate subjects: Fables,* moral considerations, drawings* for masks, and architectural and urban plans, thereby covering the vast range of activities on which the artist exercised his genius during his time at Ludovico Sforza's court.

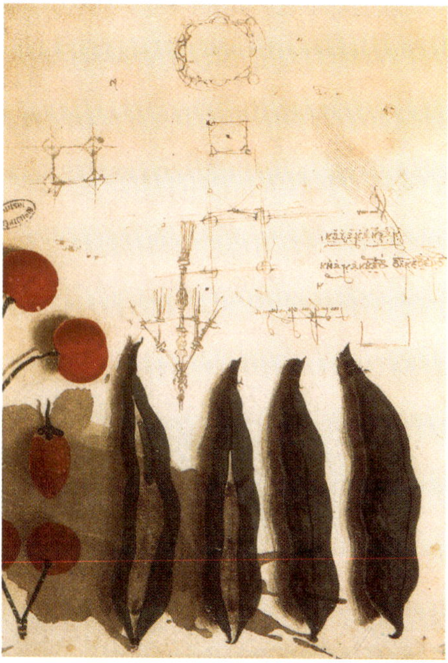

Fruit, vegetables, and architectural drawings, *Codex B*, Bibliothèque de l'Institut de France, Paris.

Codices of the Institut de France

The twelve bound or boxed manuscript* sets now in the Institute de France were in Milan's* Biblioteca Ambrosiana before Napoleon requisitioned and sent them to Paris in 1795. Late in the eighteenth century Abbot Giovan Battista Venturini devised the classification of their pages, with the letters A through M, which is still used today. The manuscript pages are smaller than those of most in other manuscript collections, and Leonardo's original organization of pages has not been disturbed. *Codex A* was written between 1490 and 1492 and is mainly concerned with movement, both as a physical science and a representational problem. *Codex B* dates from 1487 to 1489 and addresses both engineering and military architectural topics. *Codex C* is devoted to the complex matter of light and shadow, and *Codex D*, which was completed in about 1491, contains Leonardo's most consistent notes on optics and its applications in the visual arts. *Codex E* is one of the latest manuscripts. It contains notes on physical mechanics and the flight of birds with a view towards the invention of a flying machine (see *Codex on the Flight of Birds*). Leonardo's obsession with water is evident throughout *Codex F* (1508) which also contains reflections on astronomy and geometry. *Codex G* is divided into two parts. The first section is a treatise on botany, including pictorial representations of plants, written in 1510 to 1511. The second dates to 1515 and is devoted to a wide variety of subjects. Of particular interest is the project for a mirror with military applications. *Codex H* (1493–94) again manifests Leonardo's interest in water; it also contains fables* and brief moral allegories. *Codex I* is particularly heterogeneous in its subject matter, including Turkish language cryptograms. The three bound volumes comprising *Codex K* (c. 1503–07) are all devoted to geometry and *Codex L* (1497–1504) opens with preparatory notes for the *Last Supper,** followed by the development of military and civilian projects. *Codex M* dates from 1499 to 1500. It reveals Leonardo's unending passion for geometry and physics, and contains depictions of bridges, including one by Bramante.*

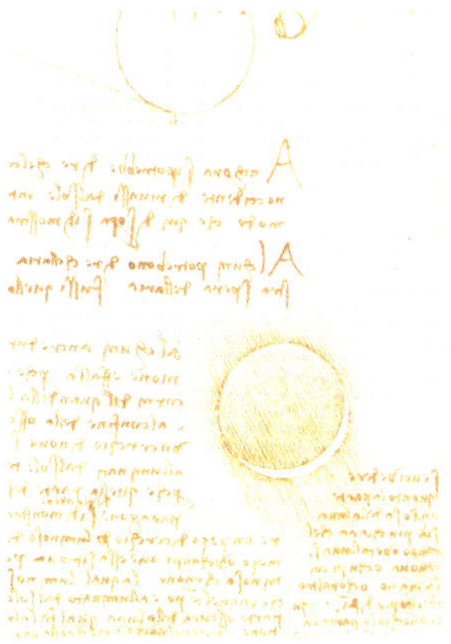

Study of the moon's luminosity, *Codex Leister,* fol. 2 r. Collection of William H. Gates III, Seattle.

Codex Leister

This manuscript* is also referred to as the *Codex Hammer* and the *Codex Gates.* It is comprised of eighteen recto-verso pages with drawings* and notes in ink. Leonardo worked on it between 1506 and 1510. He folded the pages over each other like a book, which made it easily transportable and convenient for the attachment of additions and corrections. It is possible that Leonardo intended to have it sewn together when he finished, but it has remained in a state of separate pages. Its history is well known. In 1537 the manuscript belonged to Guglielmo della Porta, a Milanese sculptor active in Rome.* The painter Giuseppe Ghezzi acquired it around 1690 and sold it to Thomas Coke, the future duke of Leicester, in 1717. It remained in that family's residence until 1980 when the American billionaire Armand Hammer purchased it. Bill Gates bought it at auction in 1994. The manuscript's main subject is water, of which Leonardo studies the movements in a fascinating series of drawings of whirlpools and converging currents. Astronomy is also taken up within this codex—a century later Leonardo's observations on the lighting of the earth and moon would be confirmed by Galileo. But water is the main focus, as when Leonardo endeavors to

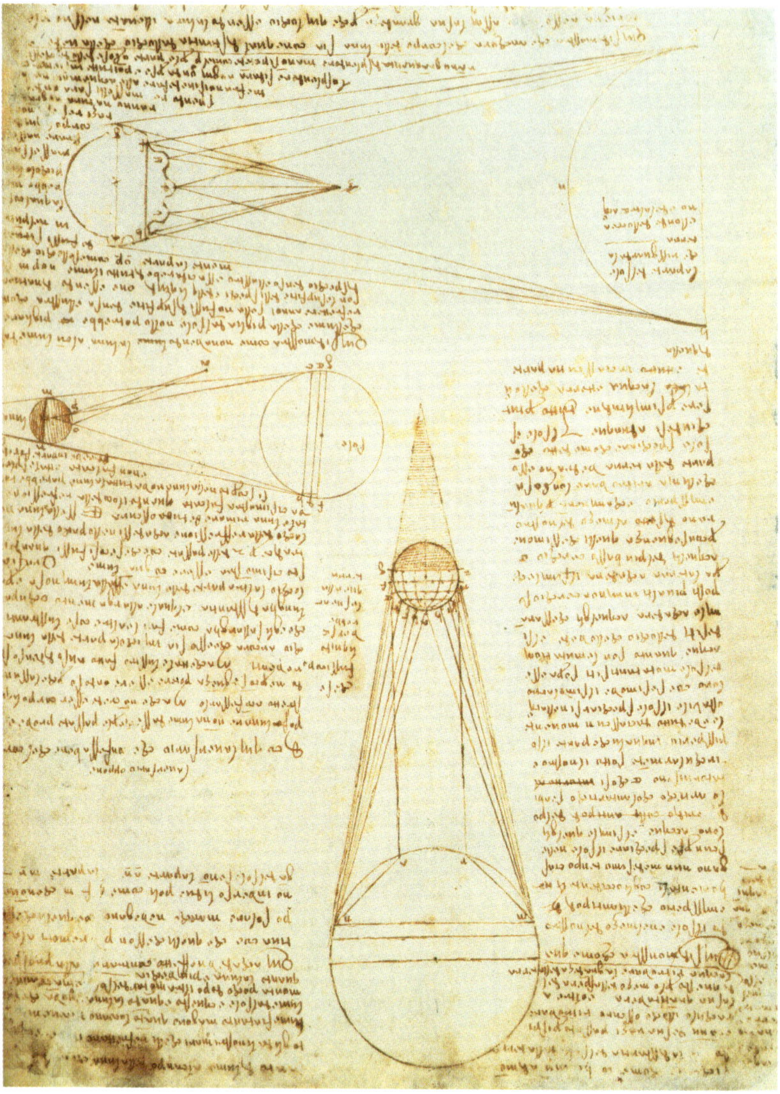

Study of the size of the earth and moon and their relation to the son, *Codex Leister,* fol. 1 r. Collection of William H. Gates III, Seattle.

explain changes caused by water on the surface of the earth. Water's erosive effects destroy, modify, stratify and, according to Leonardo, would eventually flood the planet and return it to its original state. His study of fossils led him to conclude that the earth was originally covered with water and that a gradual lowering of its levels allowed mountains and valleys to appear. This leads one to think of the mist-bathed landscapes in the backgrounds of his paintings, the *Mona Lisa* foremost among them. For Leonardo painting constituted the supreme form of human knowledge, and he constantly establishes analogies between scientific research and artistic practice.

Codex Madrid

The history of these codices contains a number of mysteries but it seems likely that they were in the possession of one Don Juan Espina early in the seventeenth century. Espina apparently acquired them in Madrid from the heirs of Pompeo Leoni and refused to turn the manuscripts* over to Lord Arundel because it was his intention to present them to the king of Spain. They did make their way into the royal collection, at the latest upon Espina's death. In any event, they are mentioned in the Spanish royal inventory of 1831 to 1833. Mislabeling during their transfer to the Royal Library (now the National Library) led to their having been lost to all for many decades. Their rediscovery in 1966 had important repercussions for our understanding of Leonardo and his work and led to hopes that additional codices might be uncovered as well. *Codex Madrid I*, as it is known, mostly contains Leonardo's notes and research from the 1490s but also contains entries and remarks dating to as late as 1508. *Madrid I* has two parts. The first contains extremely complicated plans and studies in mechanics, including magnificent and detailed drawings* of clockworks. The second contains investigations into problems in theoretical mechanics such as movement, resistance, and hydrology. *Codex Madrid II* also contains two chronologically and thematically different parts. The first was compiled between 1503 and 1505 and includes plans for military fortifications in Piombino, a canal project designed to tame the violent rising of the Arno River and to lead to economic developments for Florence,* as well as military engineering designs. Most importantly it contains interesting notes on optics and a list of books from which researchers have sought to reconstruct Leonardo's library. On the artistic front it contains notes concerning the *Battle of Anghiari*. The second part of *Madrid II*, composed between 1491 and

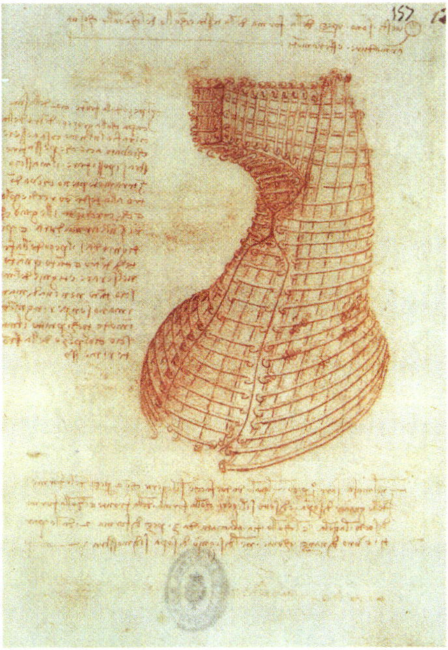

Study for an equestrian sculpture, *Codex Madrid*, fol. 57 r. Pen and ink on paper. Biblioteca Nacional, Madrid.

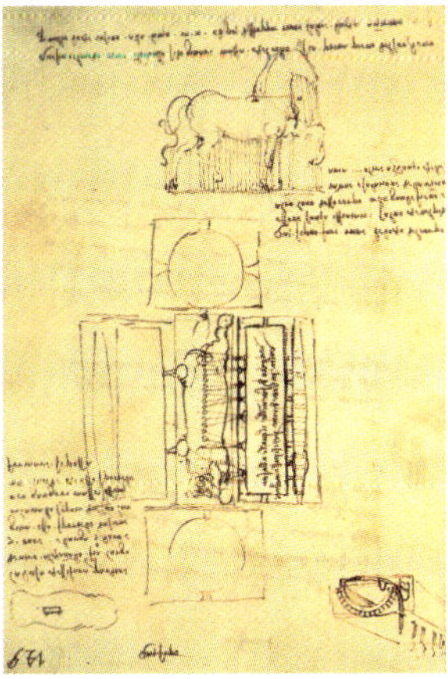

Study for a horse and other figures, *Codex Madrid*, fol. 149 r. Pen and ink on paper. Biblioteca Nacional, Madrid.

1493, contains the definitive plans for the equestrian monument honoring Francesco Sforza (see Sculpture), including precise indications on casting it in bronze.

Codex Trivulziano

This codex originally contained sixty-two sheets, some of which are now lost. It was owned by Francesco Melzi,* followed by Pompeo Leoni then, towards the beginning of the seventeenth century, Count Galeazzo Arconati, before disappearing from view until 1750. At that point Gaetano Caccia sold it to the Trivulzio family, and in 1935 it became part of the Castello Sforzesco library in Milan* along with other pieces from Prince Trivulzio's collections. An attempt to overcome and repaginate the inconsistencies of its traditional bound order has recently been undertaken. Its pages were filled between 1487 and 1490, when Leonardo was learning Latin in order to facilitate his access to humanist and scientific writings. The *Codex Trivulziano* is thus filled with notes on grammar and lexical lists (no less than fifty-one), apparently taken from the most varied sources. These lists are the fruit of an effort to obtain the most elevated literary language possible. But, apparently because Leonardo had called himself an "*uomo senza lettere*" (a man without letters), nineteenth-century specialists thought these were lists of typical and familiar Tuscan words and expressions. Still, towards the end of his life, Leonardo came to consider such efforts to be futile, as this passage from the *Codex Atlanticus** indicates: "I have such a large number of words at my disposal in my native language that I must decry my lack of perfect understanding of things rather than the lack of a vocabulary necessary to perfectly express the concepts in my mind." In addition to its linguistic exercises, the *Codex Trivulziano* includes a number of caricatures (see Anatomy and Physiognomy), as well as notes on and sketches of military and religious architecture.* The most interesting relate to the problem of the construction of the lantern of the Milan cathedral. Leonardo devoted much energy to the project without success.

Codex Windsor

Like the *Codex Atlanticus**, these 236 pages—which joined the English royal collection around 1690 after having belonged to Lord Arundel—previously belonged to Pompeo Leoni. The sculptor used scissors and glue to recompile the manuscripts* into scientific and artistic groupings. In 1994, a long and painstaking conservation effort reached the point of separating each page in order to re-compile them according to more logical chronological and thematic criteria.

The most important grouping contains some 200 anatomical* drawings* executed by Leonardo over a thirty-year period of close examination of cadavers. How he described the "human body machine" became increasingly refined over time, and reached a point of extraordinary detail and precision. About seventy sheets with landscapes are subdivided into categories (narrative landscapes, mountain studies, plant studies, waterways, symbolic landscapes, and a very impressive

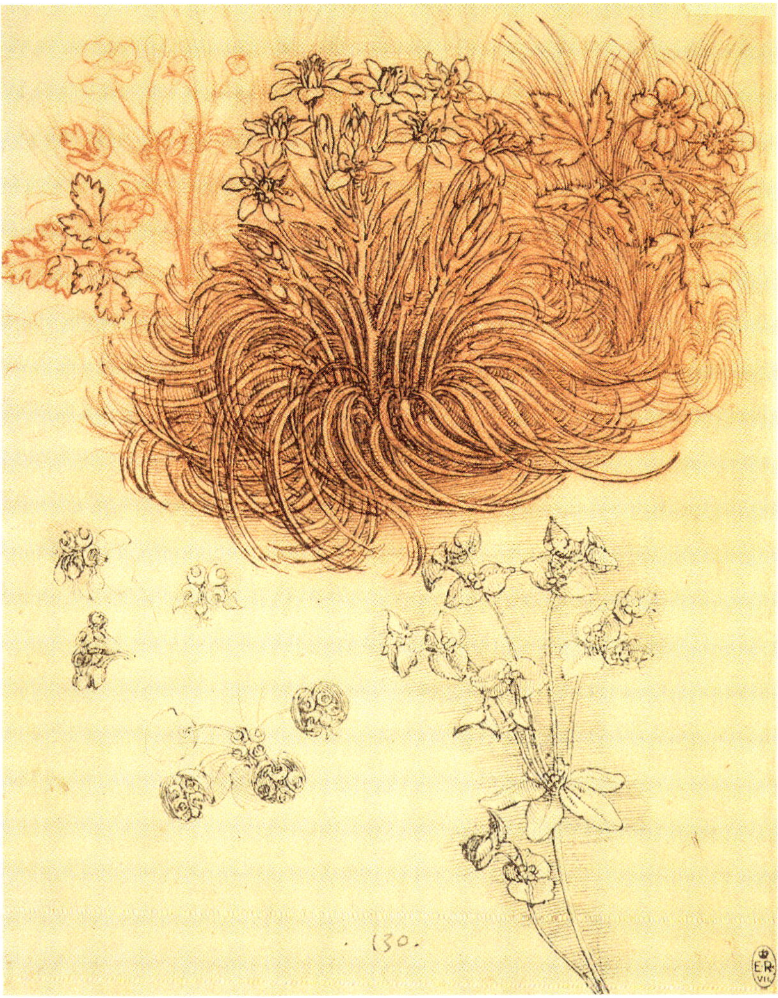

series of flood images). These studies and drawings* date to around 1513–18, and go beyond being mere reproductions of natural phenomena, to reach allegorical dimensions reflecting the artist's pessimism near the end of his life. Horses are the most common animal subjects, being preparatory studies for the *Adoration of the Magi*,* the *Battle of Anghiari* and the Sforza and Trivulzio equestrian monuments (see Sculpture). The *Codex Windsor* also includes splendid studies for the *Virgin of the Rocks** and the *Last Supper*,* as well as sketches of religious and mythological figures often done as simply exercises. Finally, a more heterogeneous grouping includes imaginary* scenes, emblems, allegories and rebuses, about twenty maps, and notes on the movement of water, architecture* and mechanics.

Star of Bethlehem and other plants, *Codex Windsor*. Red chalk and pen on paper. Windsor Castle, Royal Library.

CRITICISM

Leonardo's effort to methodically classify all questions relating to painting could not avoid indicating his tastes, along with his justifications of criteria for judging works. He was extremely critical and constantly repeated his contempt for easy solutions. Many contemporary artists paid the price of his rigor and lucidity. But the most interesting aspect of his approach combined the demand for being impersonal with a more irrational and subjective point of view. This could be seen explicitly when he employed dialogues with an imaginary antagonistic interlocutor. For example he considers that painting is meant to celebrate the beauty* of space* modeled by light and to exalt life's expressive manifestations. His opponent remarks that these two registers are not of the same order, since the first comes from pure perception and the second from psychological perception and, at any rate, modalities of expression should first be considered by the painter from a formal point of view (lines, volumes, the play of shadows, etc.). Leonardo then responds that the two aspects cannot be separated because exclusive attachment to purely visual factors without any psychological element can only lead to inexpressive geometry. According to Leonardo precisely the opposite path must be taken by animating the apparently inert forms themselves. Encounters between shadow and light, combinations of curves and straight lines, and the integration of volumes in space are the vectors of vital energy flowing through the entire natural world.

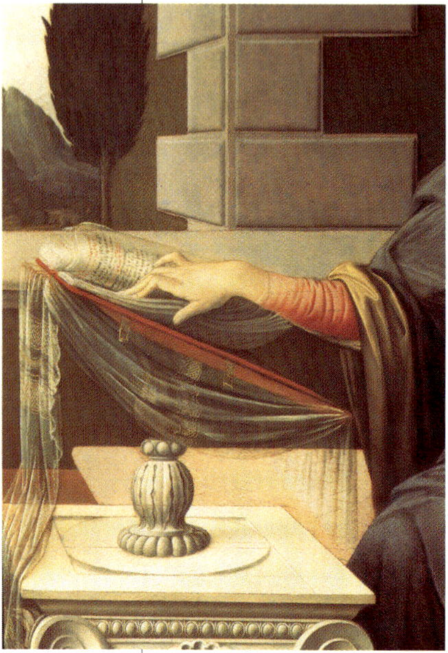

Annunciation (detail), 1472–75. Oil and tempera on wood panel. Galleria degli Uffizi, Florence.

To speak well of a base man
is much the same
as speaking ill of a good man.

(*Codex Forster II*, 41 v., Richter, 1196)

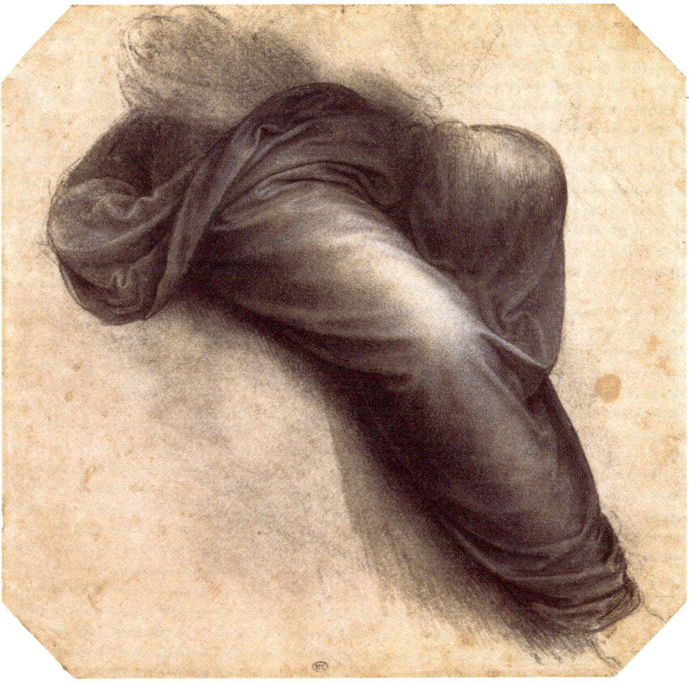

DRAWING

Leonardo was a master of the two main drawing techniques of his time, metal point and pen and ink. Most of his metal point drawings are done on prepared paper, make use of white heightening, and evidence a meticulous application of hatching techniques to create graded relief. *Studies of a Standing Horse* (c. 1490, Windsor Castle Royal Library) mark a high point in Leonardo's more than inspired draftsmanship. The rapidity of the artist's touch is evident in his earliest autograph drawing, the amazingly animated atmosphere of *Tuscan Landscape* (1473, Galleria degli Uffizi). In the drawings made in preparation for the *Adoration of the Magi** and several Virgin and Child compositions of the 1480s and early 1490s (see *Benois Madonna*, *Dreyfus Madonna*, and *Madonna of the Carnation*), Leonardo's style consistently became more swift and suggestive. His studies for the *Virgin and Child with a Cat* (c. 1478–81, British Museum, London,) describe the human body in motion with a rare degree of complexity. The energy and descriptiveness of his scientific drawings are incomparable.

Leonardo employed pen and ink in studies for paintings and sculpture, and scientific and architectural* projects. In the late 1490s his approach to shading changed significantly. He replaced hatching techniques, comprised of parallel diagonal lines, with curved marks for which shapes were determined by the form being represented. Leonardo often utilized different techniques in drawing isolated portions of larger compositions. Early in his career he produced a number of drapery studies with a fine brush and white highlights, as he had learned from Verrocchio.* (The Louvre holds a fine set of these in its graphic arts department). With the preparatory sketches of the *Last Supper** in the 1490s, he turned increasingly to less constraining, more easy to apply red and black chalks.

Drapery study for the *Virgin and Child with Saint Anne and a Lamb*. Musée du Louvre, Graphic arts department, Paris.

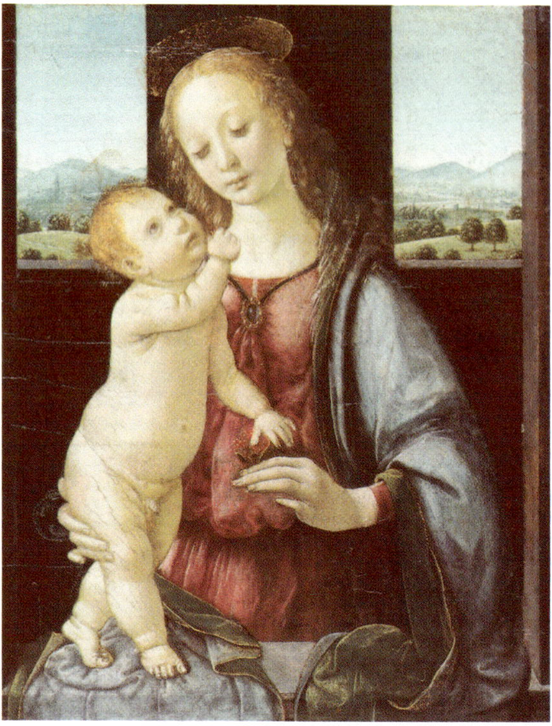

Madonna and Child with a Pomegranate, also known as the *Dreyfus Madonna,* c. 1470. Oil on wood panel, 6 ¼ × 5 ¼ in. (15.7 × 12.8 cm). National Gallery of Art, Washington.

Dreyfus Madonna

The *Dreyfus Madonna* (National Gallery of Art, Washington), also known as the *Madonna and Child with a Pomegranate,* was long attributed to Lorenzo di Credi by many experts. Most specialists now consider it the work of Leonardo. The painting has been dated to 1469–70, making it the oldest da Vinci now known. Still, it bears all the marks of a work deriving from Verrocchio's* workshop.* While it has a few regrettable aspects, such as the shortness of the Virgin's left forearm and the lack of psychological or gestural relations between the figures, its finesse, soft flesh tones and precise handling are unequaled in anything produced by Verrocchio or his disciples. The *Madonna of the Carnation* was painted very soon after the *Dreyfus Madonna* and resemblances between the two have been noted: the left hand of the Virgin, the puckering and folds of the Christ Child's right arm and the halo. The colors are also typically Leonardian, particularly the combination of red, deep green, yellow, blue, and violet; as well as white touches bringing out folds in the fabric. X-rays and infrared scans reveal that the bluish mountains were added at a later time, but are almost certainly the work of Leonardo himself. Leonardo's iconography differs radically from that of the *Madonnas* painted contemporaneously by Botticelli. By isolating the two figures, Leonardo avoids overloading the image with angels. At the same time, the figures become an exercise in formal symmetry, which gives them a much more domestic and familiar feel.

Facing page: Studies for the set decorations of Politian's "Orpheus," *Codex Arundel,* fol. 231 v. and 224 r., c. 1506–08. British Museum. London.

ENTERTAINMENTS

Organizing ceremonies and pageants were among the great number of Leonardo's duties when he worked for princely patrons.* Numerous written references to these events exist but little visual evidence relating to them has made it to our time. His manuscripts* suggest that two kinds of entertainments particularly engaged Leonardo's imagination—large official court ceremonies and designs for theatrical performances. He devised all sorts of amusing inventions for the first. These included the temporary and festive architectural structures, automata, and fountains he would create throughout his lifetime. One event for which an extremely complex series of drawings* exists is the double wedding of Ludovico and Anna Sforza to Beatrice and Alfonso d'Este in 1491. It has been noted how classical references and Christian symbolism combined to convey an array of symbolic forms making allusion to, among other things, the vicissitudes of fortune and the cardinal virtues, in a manner comparable to the rich arcane allusions of some of Leonardo's paintings, for example, the *Virgin and Child with Saint Anne and a Lamb* (Musée du Louvre). Several preparatory designs of allegorical compositions intended to celebrate the Sforza family come from that same use of a visual language with hidden meaning, as much in accord with the wishes of the sponsors as with the artist's personality.* In the domain of theater set design, Leonardo made use of his research in mechanics to create special effects with large and complex moveable machinery (see *Codex Arundel*). And as an accomplished amateur musician, he was quite capable of producing works combining actors, singers, and musicians—entertainments that would eventually give birth to opera. Writings of his contemporaries describe his set designs for the first performance of Bernardo Bellincioni's *La festa del Paradiso,* including an immense celestial hemisphere that put to use his knowledge of astronomy. He was probably paid handsomely for these entertainments, yet one cannot help but wonder how much they must have diverted the artist from finishing his paintings.

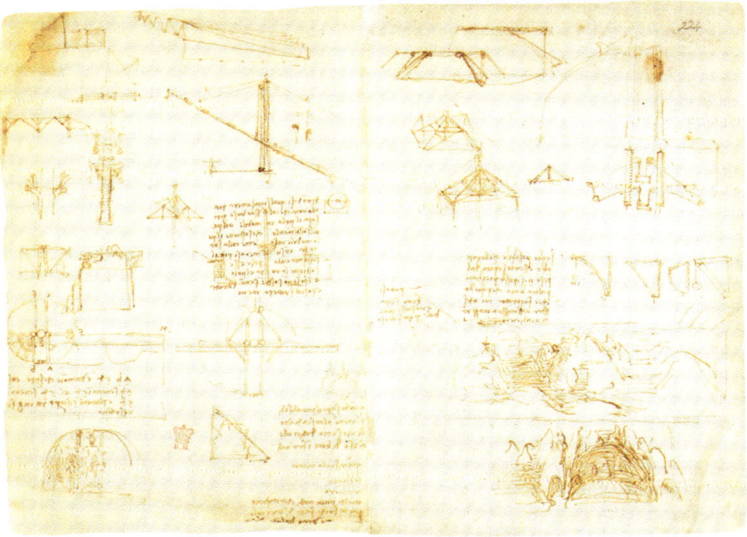

FABLES

"The vain and wandering butterfly, not content with being able to fly at its ease through the air, overcome by the tempting flame of the candle, decided to fly into it; but its sportive impulse was the cause of a sudden fall, for its delicate wings were burnt in the flame. And the hapless butterfly having dropped, all scorched, at the foot of the candlestick, after much lamentation and repentance, dried the tears from its swimming eyes, and raising its face exclaimed: O false light! how many must thou have miserably deceived in the past, like me; or if I must indeed see light so near, ought I not to have known the sun from the false glare of dirty tallow." (*Codex Atlanticus,** 67 r., Richter, 1268)

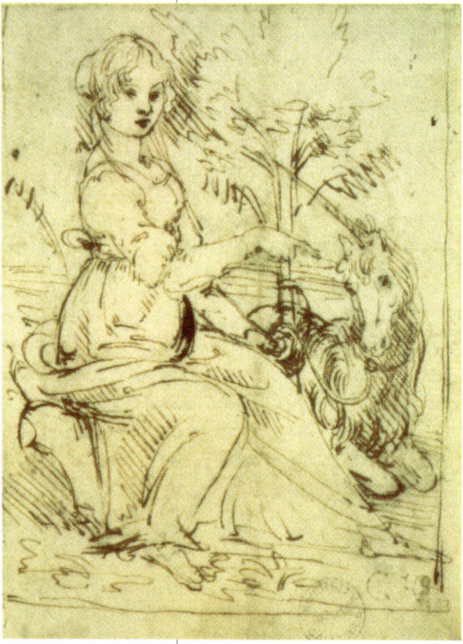

Woman with a Unicorn, c. 1480. Pen and dark brown ink. Ashmolean Museum, Oxford.

"The cedar, being desirous of producing a fine and noble fruit at its summit, set to work to form it with all the strength of its sap. But this fruit, when grown, was the cause of the tall and upright tree-top being bent over." (ibid., 67 v., Richter, 1275)

"Of Walnut trees, that are beaten: Those which have done best will be most beaten, and their offspring taken and flayed or peeled, and their bones broken or crushed." (ibid., 76 r., Richter, 1303)

"The fig-tree, having no fruit, no one looked at it; then, wishing to produce fruits that it might be praised by men, it was bent and broken down by them." (ibid., 76 r., Richter, 1303)

"The flint was shocked at the steel's impact upon it and remarked in harsh tones, 'How can you presume to torment me in this way? Stop bothering me, because you have chosen me in error, me, who has never harmed anyone.' The steel replied, 'If you are willing to be patient you will see yourself produce wonderful results.' Upon hearing these words the flint was appeased, endured the punishment and saw himself produce fire, a marvelous element that enters in the composition of innumerable things. This is said for those who feel discouraged when they begin their studies but who then apply themselves and triumph their efforts, who give themselves over to it with patience and perseverance and obtain wonderful results." (ibid., 257 r.)

Florence

It was thanks to Filippo Brunelleschi's architecture, Masaccio's painting and Donatello's sculpture, that Florence became the artistic capital of Italy fifty years before Leonardo was born. At this time the basic principles of the early Renaissance were defined and artists assumed a new role in society. Florence was at the height of its territorial expansion and had become firmly established as a republican city-state in the first half of the fifteenth century. The *Arti Maggiori,* or professional guilds, were still in charge of most major public commissions, but the aristocracy was becoming increasingly involved as patrons* of the arts. Starting with Cosimo I, the Medicis moved to make the republic into an oligarchy controlled by themselves and their allies, while using artistic commissions as more or less evident propaganda for the family. Lorenzo (il Magnifico) de' Medici dominated Florence during the last third of the Quattrocento. He was quick to realize that the most eminent Tuscan artists could be used diplomatically in his campaign for prestige. This is why he sent Leonardo to the Milan* court. But Lorenzo's strategy caused such a large number of architects, sculptors, and painters to leave Florence, that it effectively undermined his cause by leading to a decrease in Tuscan artistic production. Even in Florence, the most important commissions were not made at the behest of the Medicis, but by other aristocratic families, the clergy, and religious orders. The political situation became extremely unstable upon Lorenzo's death. Between 1494 and 1498 the Dominican monk Girolamo Savonarola held an overwhelming influence over the city. His fanatically puritanical positions struck a mortal blow to artistic creation. Until the 1530s when the Medicis returned solidly to power, instability reigned as governance alternated between the Medicis and republican governments.

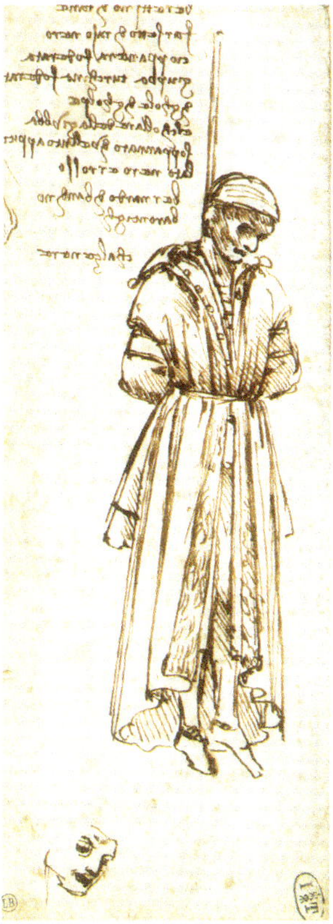

Study of a hanged man: Bernardo Baroncelli, Giuliano de' Medici's assassin, 1479. Pen and ink on paper, 7 ½ x 3 in. (19.2 x 7.8 cm). Musée Bonnat, Bayonne.

Leonardo, Michelangelo, and Raphael were all in Florence during the first decade of the sixteenth century. The first two artists were effectively made to compete by the public authorities at the time when Leonardo was commissioned to paint the *Battle of Anghiari* (see Introduction). The much younger Raphael used his prodigious

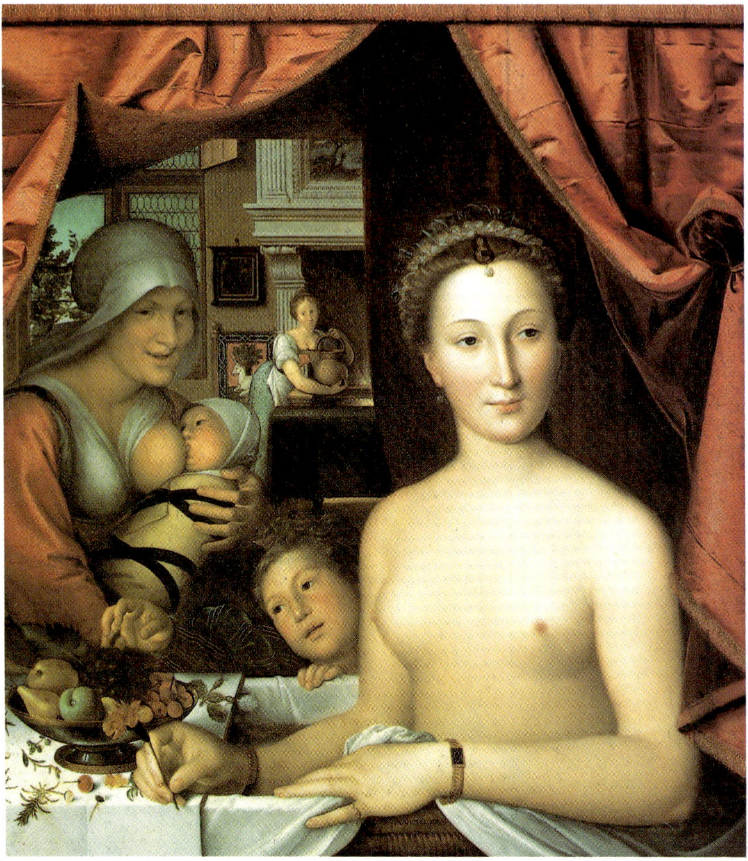

François Clouet, *Lady in her Bath,* c. 1570. Oil on wood panel, 3 ft. ½ × 2 ft. 8 in. (93 × 81 cm). National Gallery of Art, Washington.

intelligence to assimilate the inventions of his elders. The presence in Florence of these three geniuses marked the beginning of the High Renaissance, and gave the city back its role as the artistic center of the Italian peninsula. But that position was gradually lost to Rome* and Venice.*

France

Leonardo spent the last three years of his life in France, where he died. King Francis I appreciated his abilities in all domains and offered him excellent conditions for pursuing his research and artistic pursuits. Leonardo apparently came to France with the *Mona Lisa,** *Saint John the Baptist,** the *Virgin and Child with Saint Anne and a Lamb,* and *Leda and the Swan,* where he brought them to their final state of completion. The range of subjects and projects he worked on was great, from court entertainments* to architectural* plans for a royal residence at Romorantin to the series of drawings, *A Deluge,* now in the Windsor Castle Royal Library. Despite his tremendous reputation in France and his standing vis-à-vis the court, his influence* on French artists is difficult to establish and seems most often limited to superficial thematic or formal citations. For example, figures from the *Virgin of the Rocks** have been used as models with various degrees of Italianate and Flemish accents in church altarpieces and miniatures. Beginning with Francis I's tapestry copy of the *Last Supper,** French painters have sought to learn lessons on facial expression and physical gesture from Leonardo. Some of the most interesting results can be seen in the paintings of Jean, François, and Polet Clouet. The subject matter, facial expression, and contours in Jean Clouet's *Portrait of Francis I as Saint John the Baptist* (1518, private collection) owe a great deal to Leonardo, as do the hatching techniques he employs in his drawings. In the middle of the century, his son François inaugurated a new Leonardism by returning to Leonardo's themes and varying his balance between naturalism and idealism, in *Bath of Diana* (Musée des Beaux-Arts, Rouen) and *Lady in her Bath* (National Gallery of Art, Washington). Polet Clouet was most likely Jean's brother and the probable author of a portrait in which a parrot is perched on the subject's right hand, known as *The Parrot Portrait* (Walker Art Gallery, Liverpool) and thought to be of Marguerite de Navarre, Francis I's sister. The painting has been called "the French Mona Lisa" by the art historian Cécile Scaillíérez.

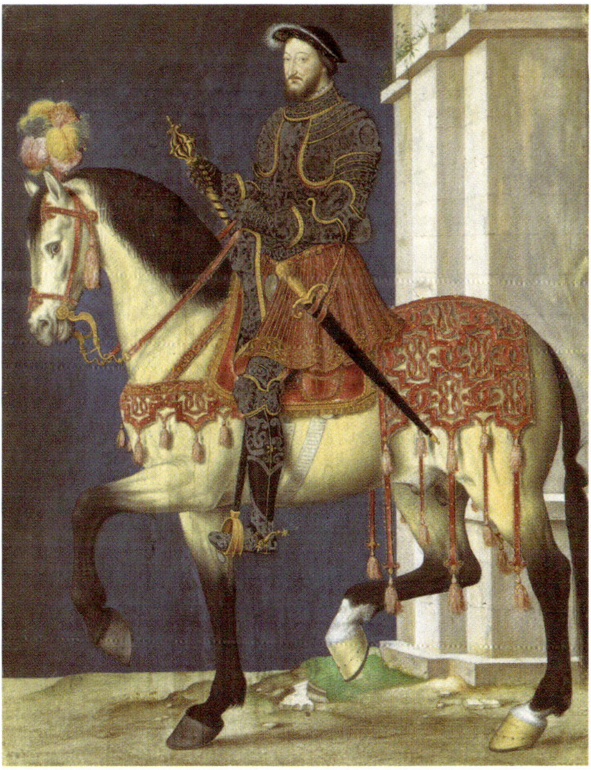

François Clouet, *Portrait of Francis I, King of France,* 1540. Gouache on parchment and wood panel. Musée du Louvre, Paris.

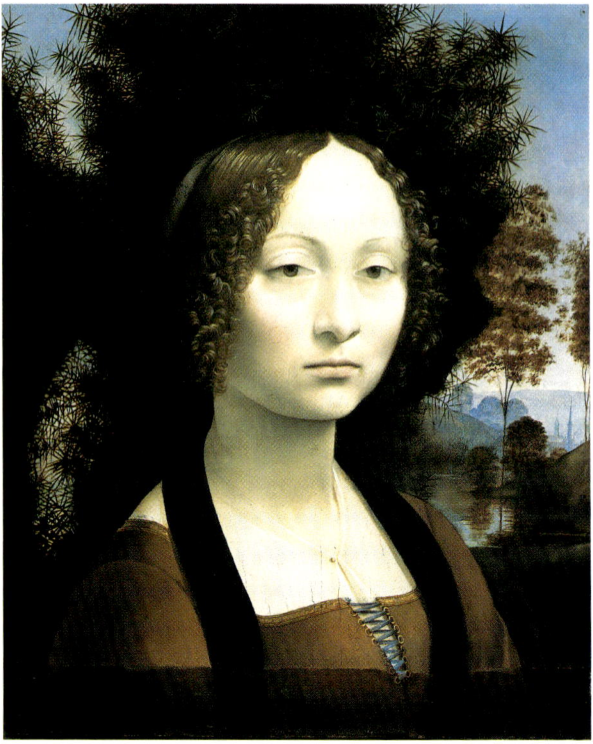

Ginevra Benci, c. 1474. Tempera and oil on wood panel, 15 × 14 ½ in. (38.5 × 36.7 cm). National Gallery of Art, Washington.

Gaddiano, Anonimo

In 1545 or so, a Tuscan writer known as Anonimo Gaddiano (or Magliabechiano Anonimo) completed a *Life of Leonardo da Vinci.* We know nothing about the author. But like other biographers such as Paolo Giovio* and Vasari* he seemed to be fascinated by Leonardo's many talents: "While Leonardo da Vinci, a Florentine citizen, was the natural son of Ser Piero da Vinci, he was of noble origin on his mother's side. He was so exceptional and his capacities so universal that one could say that his birth was a miracle of nature. Not only did nature bless him with exceptional physical beauty, but she also made him beyond comparison in a multitude of other qualities. He was extremely competent in mathematics and perspective (see *Sfumato*), he was a sculptor,* and excelled beyond all in drawing.* His inventions were numerous, but he did not manage to apply color to many of his paintings, because he was never satisfied with them, and his works are rare. He spoke eloquently, played the lyre exceptionally well and taught that art to Atalante Migliorotti. He was interested and took pleasure in botany, and was expert in the domains of artillery, waterworks, fountains, and other remarkable inventions (see Entertainments). His mind was never at rest and he continually created ingenious inventions." Gaddiano then goes on to inform us, "In his youth, he was employed by Lorenzo il Magnifico. He employed Leonardo for work on a garden for Saint Mark's Square in Florence."* This probably refers to restoration of ancient statues, another indication of Leonardo's early interest in sculpture. Unfortunately the rest of this short biography is too disorganized and riddled with inaccuracies to be considered a serious source. The list of works at the end of the account however is a useful tool for historical restorations and it describes many no longer extant paintings and sculptures.

Ginevra Benci

It is not known how Leonardo came into contact with the Benci family, but his relationship with them lasted into the first decade of the sixteenth century; *Saint John the Baptist** was commissioned by another member of the family, Giovanni Benci. Before being unanimously credited to Leonardo by modern specialists, the portrait of *Ginevra Benci* (National Gallery of Art, Washington) had been attributed to Lucas Cranach, Verrocchio,* Domenico Ghirlandaio, and Lorenzo di Credi. Some experts date it to 1474, the year Ginevra was married to Luigi di Bernardo di Lapo Nicolini. More recent specialists believe that it was executed in 1475 or 1476 at the behest of Bernardo Bembo, the Venetian* ambassador to Florence.* Bembo, in the neoplatonist* manner of the Medici court, was apparently attached to Ginevra Benci with a strong platonic love. Stylistically, the painting exhibits a combination of sculptural modeling techniques learned from Verrocchio* and Leonardo's own experiments. It is likely that he sought to compete with Flemish models, and particularly with van Eyck, from whom he seems to have borrowed the technique of highlighting the curls of hair on either side of Ginevra's face. Modern technical analysis has revealed the process Leonardo used to achieve the melancholy expression and the amazingly life-like skin tones: he blurred the layers of paint by working it with his fingers. The contrast between the marble-like impassability of the almost bloodless face and bust, and the treatment of the vegetation bursting with life is striking. The branches of the juniper tree (an allusion to the model's name) and the trees on the right in the background seem to be moved by a soft breeze. The reverse side of the panel is painted with intertwined branches set against a *faux* porphyry background with the motto, *Virtutem forma decorat* (beauty adorns virtue). Such combinations of allegory and portraiture became extremely popular among sixteenth-century artists, particularly the Tuscan Mannerists in Venice.*

Giovio, Paolo

Like Anonimo Gaddiano* and Vasari,* the Italian humanist Paolo Giovio (1483–1552) compiled a series of writings on

Anatomical studies, *Codex Windsor*. Windsor Castle, Royal Library.

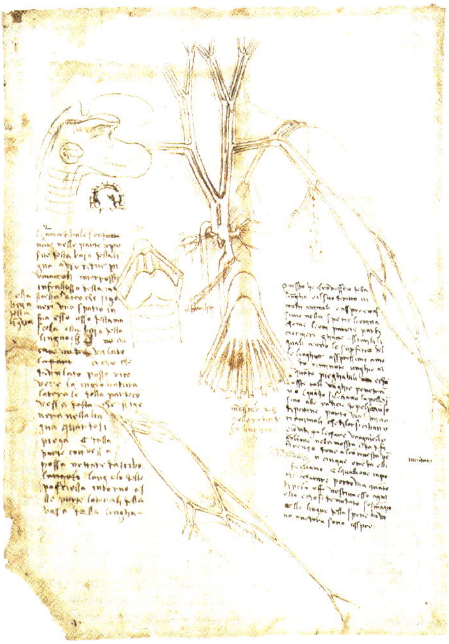

illustrious men of his time. His extensive narrative work is called *Histories of His Own Times* and his first brief biographical mention of Leonardo dates to 1527. Despite its brevity and minor errors of fact, his account is important for its recognition of the link between art and science.* "Leonardo, who was born in the humble Tuscan village of Vinci, brought brilliance to painting. He proved that the art of painting could only be correctly exercised by those who practiced the sciences and higher disciplines, and that these are indispensable to that art." Giovio provides details concerning how Leonardo worked. "He considered modeling more important than brushwork in works on a flat surface. In his view, nothing was more important than optics (see *Sfumato*) since it allowed him to render deliberately the distribution of light and shadow in the smallest details. He also went to medical schools to learn dissection on the bodies of criminals, despite the inhuman and disgusting character of this work, in order to paint the flexing and exertions of different members according to the action of muscles and the natural order of

HISTORICAL RECEPTION

Leonardo's greatness has been recognized through the centuries. But how his work has been seen and understood has differed over time, and it has suffered from erroneous attributions. His position as founder of the High Renaissance was established by virtue of the eminent status accorded to him by Vasari.* At the beginning of the third part of *Lives of the Artists,* Vasari presents what remained the dominant interpretation of Leonardo's artistic personality* at least until the nineteenth century. Cassiano dal Pozzo, the great seventeenth-century connoisseur, collector, and patron of the arts collaborated with Count Galeazzo Arconati to develop a new perspective on Leonardo. Although the efforts of these two great Roman* collectors to bring Leonardo's manuscripts* to publication were unsuccessful, Cassiano did provide Paul Fréart de Chambray with the material he eventually brought to France and published as the *Treatise on Painting** (1651, including illustrations by Nicolas Poussin). In the seventeenth and eighteenth centuries, critical perspectives on Leonardo were partially shaped by incorrect attributions and incomplete knowledge of the extent of his work. However, significant advances were made towards the turn of the twentieth century. Efforts were made to publish the surviving manuscripts and scholarly attention was applied to establish a chronology of the artist's career based on solid evidence. From that point on there has been a large and steady flow of writings on Leonardo, some of it excellent, some of it less so. The best studies have elucidated Leonardo's position in European art and clarified various aspects of his protean mind. The first really innovative synthetic work on Leonardo was published by Kenneth Clark in 1935 and a number of significant monographs as well as translations, studies, catalogues, facsimile editions, and articles, have appeared since the 1950s (see Bibliography).

joints (see Anatomy and Physiognomy). He engraved the forms of all these elements onto blocks, including the smallest veins and the inside of bones, in order that innumerable copies be stamped for the benefit of art." Giovio also included a traditional criticism* of the artist. "But because he spent his time exploring the difficult regions of art, his versatile mind and his natural inconsistency (see Personality) always led him to put off the execution of his work and thus he produced few works." Finally, Giovio offers a description of Leonardo's gifts and their effects on his contemporaries: "He was affable, brilliant, generous, had an extremely attractive face, and since he was a wonderful arbiter and inventor of all sorts of amusements and distinguished diversions, especially court entertainments,* and an expert singer who accompanied himself on the lyre, he was very dear to all the princes of the time." (See Patrons.)

Humor

"A priest, making the rounds of his parish on Easter Eve, and sprinkling holy water in the houses as is customary, came to

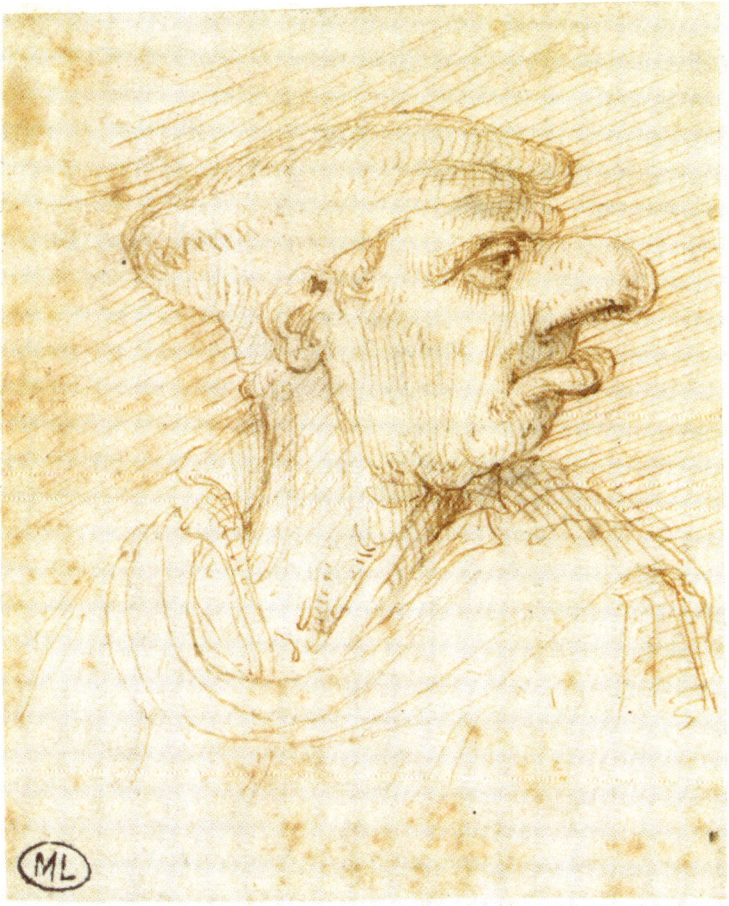

Leonardo da Vinci (?), caricature. Musée du Louvre, Graphic arts department, Paris.

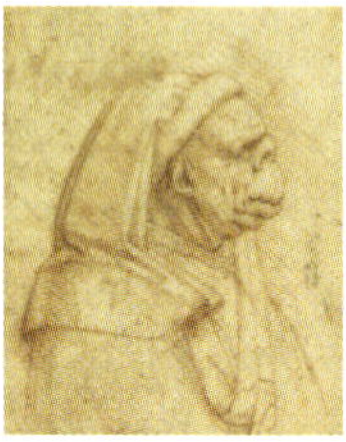

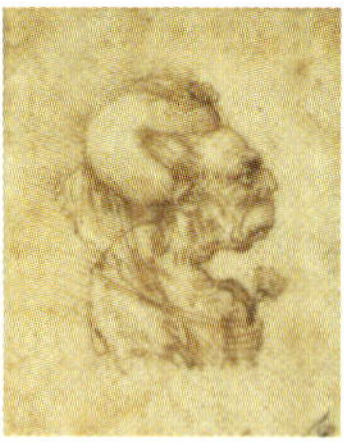

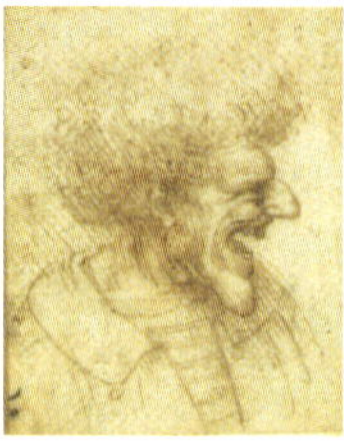

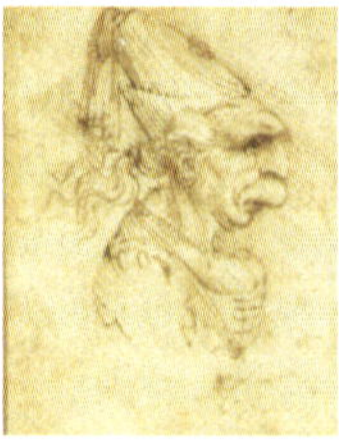

Four caricatures. Christie's Images, London.

a painter's room, where he sprinkled the water on some of his pictures. The painter turned round, somewhat angered, and asked him why this sprinkling had been bestowed on his pictures; then said the priest, that it was the custom and his duty to do so, and that he was doing good; and that he who did good might look for good in return and, indeed, for better, since God had promised every good deed that was done on earth should be rewarded a hundred-fold from above. Then the painter, waiting till he went out, went to an upper window and flung a large pail of water on the priest's back, saying: 'Here is the reward a hundred-fold from above, which you said would come from the good you had done me with your holy water, by which you have damaged my pictures.'" (*Codex Atlanticus*,*119 r., Richter, 1280)

"A man wishing to prove, by the authority of Pythagoras, that had formerly been in the world, while another would not let him finish his argument, the first speaker said to the second: 'It is by this token that I was formerly here, I remember that you were a miller.' The other one, feeling himself stung by these words, agreed that it was true, and that by the same token he remembered that the speaker had been the ass that carried the flour." (*Codex M*, Institut de France, 58 v., Richter, 1285)

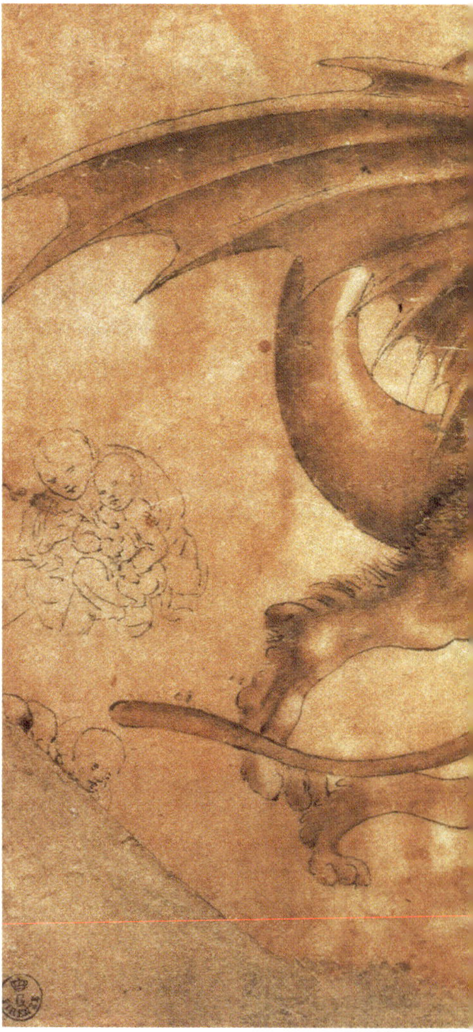

It was asked of a painter why, since he made such beautiful figures, which were but dead things, his children were so ugly; to which the painter replied that he made his pictures by day, and his children by night." (ibid.)

"A man was desired to rise from bed, because the sun was already risen. To which he replied: 'If I had as far to go, and as much to do as he has, I should be risen by now; but having but a little way to go, I shall not rise yet.'" (*Codex Forster** II, 31 r., Richter, 1291)

Imaginary Scenes

Between Leonardo's ambition to express through his painting the absolute truth of the universe, and his paintings that were actually completed, there lies a vast domain where the creatures of dreams stimulate

Battle between a dragon and a lion. Brown ink over wash. Galleria degli Uffizi, Gabinetto Disegni e Stampe, Florence.

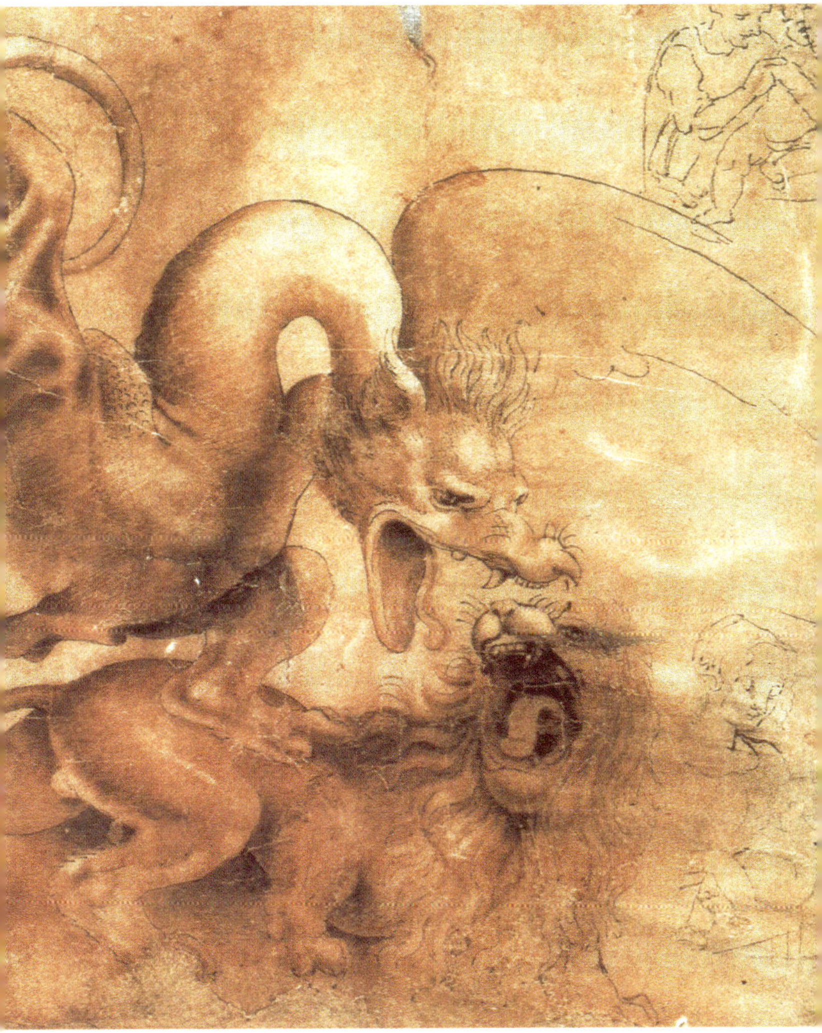

the imagination. Leonardo's writings and drawings* indicate that he returned to such realms more and more frequently and with ever increasing passion.
Such imaginary scenes must have been born out of Leonardo's need to resolve specific problems that came up in the execution of his other works. But the imaginary scenes came to develop into a domain of their own, separate from the traditional imagery of religious and profane iconography.
In fact, starting with the *Virgin of the Rocks,** Leonardo's paintings were the expression of a compromise between the exigencies of a particular theme and his aspiration for a "total" art.
It shouldn't be surprising then, if while complementing his works with an extensive collection of drawings, that Leonardo also set about to justify and elaborate on their validity in writing. Thus descriptions and stories appear in his manuscripts* detailing imaginary subjects such as the "terrible giants of Libya" (*Codex Atlanticus** 311 r. and 96 v.; Richter, 1354), "Mount Taurus and Mount Atlas" (ibid., 214 r., Richter, 1354) or the "Island of Venus" (*Codex Windsor,** 2591 r. v., Richter, 1104)
These imaginary developments are not fables,* which are also found in his notebooks. They should probably be considered exercises for the acuity of visual imagination.
His fantastical literary explorations of impossible fleeting scenes are useful for deciphering their visual analogues, and keeping images of visual imagination from fading away. These scenes present the ironic revenge of the word over the image written by the artist who consistently argued for the superiority of painting over poetry (see Paragone).

From the shore of the Southern coast of Cilicia may be seen to the South the beautiful island of Cyprus, which was the realm of the goddess Venus, and many navigators being attracted by her beauty, had their ships and rigging broken amidst the reefs, surrounded by the whirling waters. Here the beauty of delightful hills tempts wandering mariners to refresh themselves amidst their flowery verdure, where the winds are tempered and fill the island and the surrounding seas with fragrant odours.

(*Codex Windsor*, 2591 r. v., Richter, 1104)

Facing page: Agnolo Bronzino, *Holy Family*. Oil on wood panel. Musée du Louvre, Paris.

INFLUENCE

Every aspect of sixteenth-century Italian art was directly or indirectly affected by Leonardo's innovations, and the same holds true for most of Europe. All of his major narrative paintings contributed significantly to the evolution of the history-painting genre. The influence of his religious paintings was immense. His portraits established new criteria, the search for profound psychological evocation of the sitter and sophisticated compositional plans; as can be witnessed in the work of Bronzino. Most of his discoveries were diffused throughout Europe through copies, variants, and pastiches. The very free style he employed in his sketches and studies (see Drawing) strongly influenced his Italian successors, most radically the work of Raphael, but also his great rival, Michelangelo.

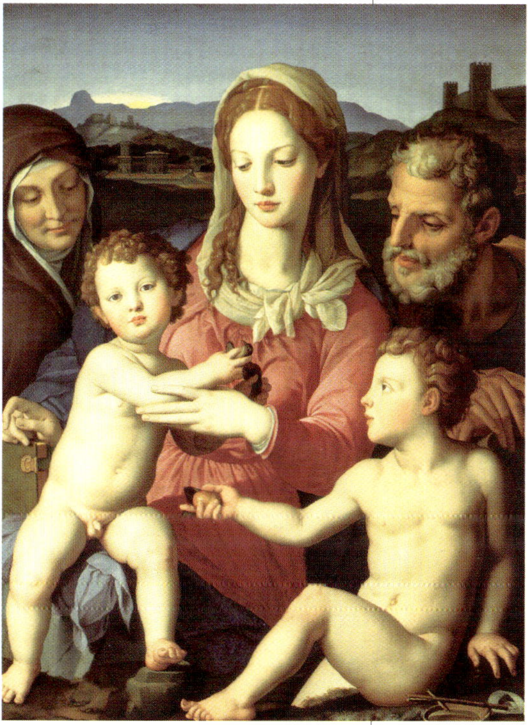

No artist following Leonardo attained the levels of simultaneously precise and soft modeling as he did by shadowing and lighting both objects and human figures. As Vasari* put it, his *sfumato** techniques brought the end of the "dry" manner of Quattrocento painting. Leonardo's influence on sculpture,* architecture,* and court entertainments* is more difficult to distinguish, considering the dearth of works in these domains that have survived to our time. While his scientific research, which delved so deeply into so many areas, remained beyond the purview of his contemporaries as well as his successors, his theories* were in broad circulation among academic circles, even if an edition of the *Treatise on Painting** was not published until 1651. His influence on the iconography of European art has been tremendous, from the respectful interpretations of Antoine Watteau, to Marcel Duchamp's more playfully iconoclastic responses.

LADY WITH AN ERMINE

This painting—previously attributed to Boltraffio* and Giovanni Ambrogio de Predis* and sometimes referred to as the *Portrait of Cecilia Gallerani* (Czartoryski Muzeum, Krakow)—is now unanimously considered to be the work of Leonardo. Recently discovered documents have enabled it to be dated between approximately 1488 and 1490. Ludovico Sforza most probably commissioned the portrait, and it was during the same time period that he was most intensely involved with this young woman, with whom he had an illegitimate son and to whom he deeded lands.

From a stylistic perspective, the objectivity of anatomical rendering—particularly notable in the right hand—links the painting to scientific drawings Leonardo was making in his notebooks at the time. As far as its tones are concerned, the chromatic combinations are similar to those of Leonardo's second *Virgin of the Rocks.** In this painting, compared to *The Musician** of c. 1485, we find Leonardo even more masterfully controlling the construction of space.

The intensity of detail (even with portions of the image in a poor state of conservation) and the dynamism of the pose shape the young woman and the animal into an energetic image of fluid and elegant curves that is precisely the opposite of the usual stiff portrait styles of the era. The articulation of the subject in space is extremely complex, and translates most aptly Leonardo's theory* about physical disposition and demeanor as the visual expression of invisible "movements of the soul." The model appears to have just turned her attention to something or someone to the right of the picture frame, lending an impression of reality to the image—something rarely achieved by fifteenth-century Florentine painters. A rhythm of light and dark zones serves to animate the image and define volume. The Codices* of the Institut de France (*Codex C*) contain drawings and notes comprising a detailed study of how light hits different solid objects and how a great variety of shadow effects appear; they were used in preparation for a chapter on the topic in the *Treatise on Painting.** Such illusionistic effects as the straight lines of pearls partially in light and partially in shadow, which themselves cause a shadow on the skin and dress, expertly multiply the visual possibilities.

Lady with an Ermine, c. 1488–90. Oil on wood panel, 20 ⅞ x 15 ½ in. (54.8 x 40.3). Czartoryski Muzeum, Krakow.

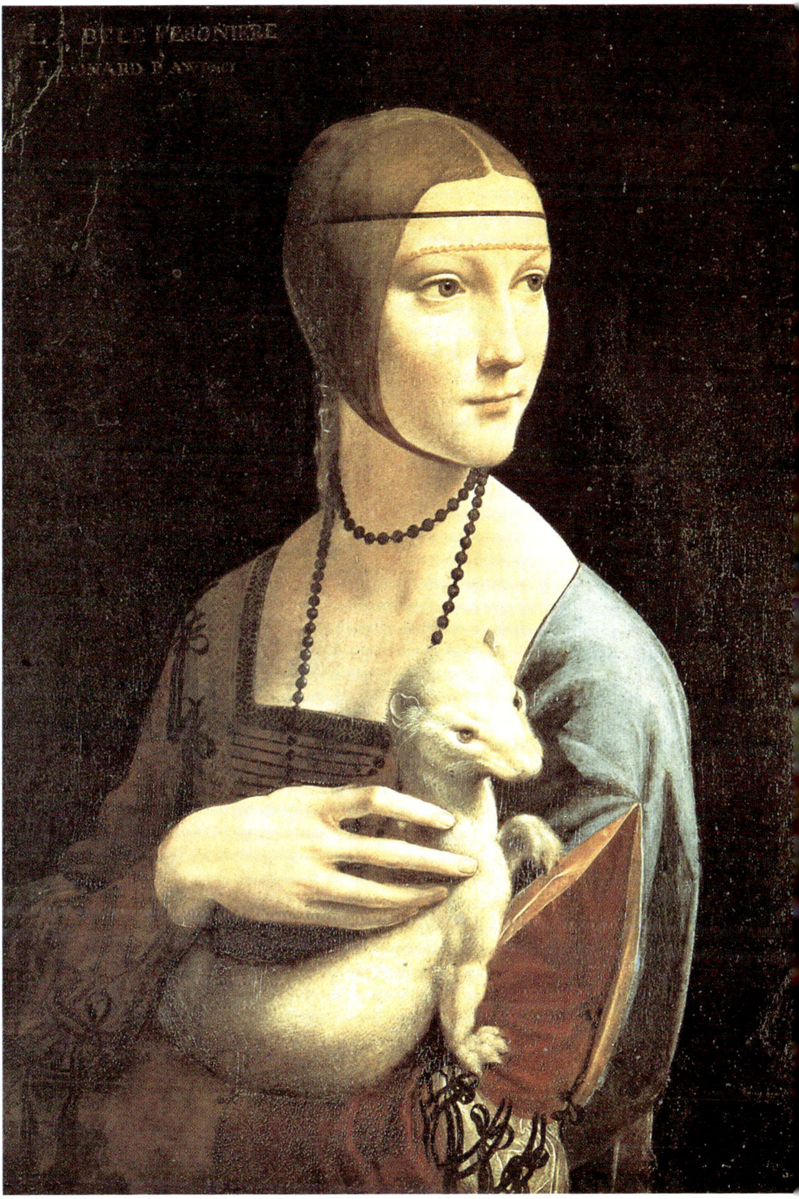

LAST SUPPER

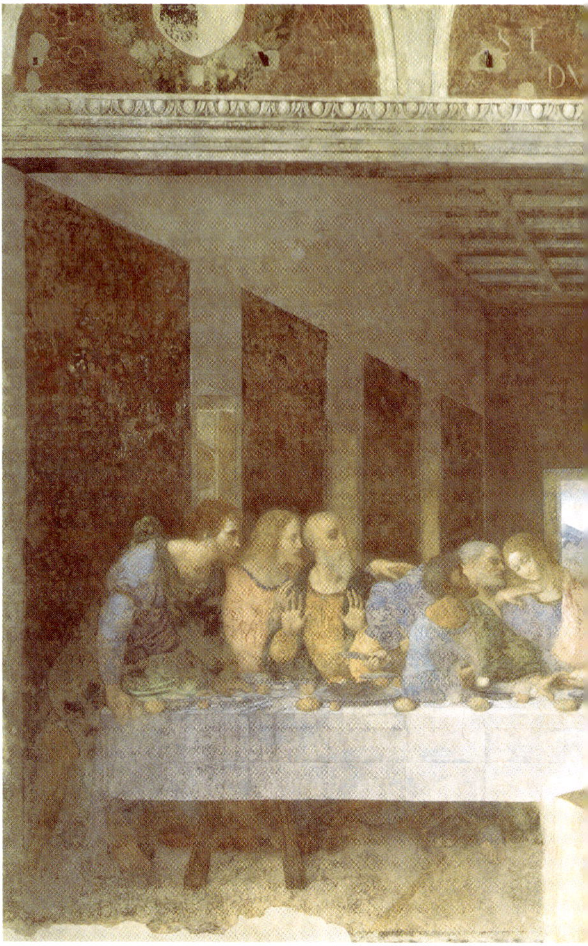

Last Supper, 1494–98 (after restoration). Tempera and oil on two preparatory layers, 13 ft. 10 × 29 ft. 7 ½ in. (4.60 × 8.8 m). Santa Maria delle Grazie, Milan.

Even if it is sometimes argued that this work was accomplished in collaboration with his students, the attribution of the *Last Supper* (Santa Maria delle Grazie, Milan) to Leonardo has never been disputed. The recent restoration (1978–99) has enabled numerous parts done by his own hand to be identified, particularly the traces of finishing touches (gold, violet, and white highlights) of exceptional quality. The execution of this work began in 1494 and extended to 1498 when the humanist Luca Pacioli announced its completion. Rather than using traditional fresco techniques, Leonardo used tempera, embellished here and there with glazes, over two dry preparatory layers. This enabled him to work in conformity with his habits at a less pressing pace, and most importantly, to obtain amazing transparent and reflecting effects. The synthesis in his painting of the artistic and scientific activities he pursued in Milan* of anatomical,* mechanical, physiognomic and optical (see *Sfumato*) principles, to a large-scale production, probably took some inspiration from Bramante's* architectural projects. The illusionism of the spatial construction is the result of rigorous application of the rules of

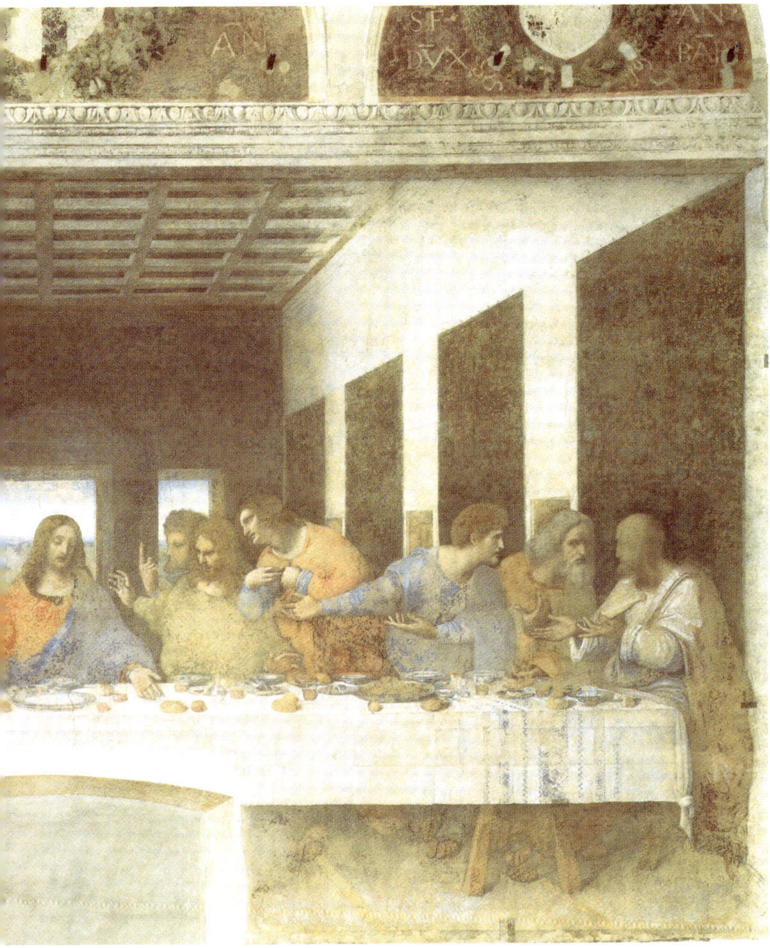

perspective—which make the painting appear to be a continuation of the real space of the refectory—and also the result of lighting effects; the large figures of the apostles are brightly lit so as to give them the maximum relief possible. The distribution of shadow (of which every possible nuance is explored, from full, to biased, to colored) gives the viewer the impression that the scene is lit only by light from the room's windows and three openings in the background of the painted architecture. Leonardo concentrates Christ's announcement of Judas' betrayal and the establishment of the Eucharist, into a single, intensely dramatic moment. The apostles are deftly arranged into groups of three, in a composition presenting echoes and symmetry, but with none of the figures repeating exactly the same pose, and all the while appearing perfectly natural. Each character has a different expression and physical position as he expresses a well-defined and nuanced reaction to what has just been revealed. The composition's movement and vitality, the beauty of some of the faces, and the many virtuoso flourishes, such as the still-life on the table, have fed the imagination of other great artists, with Caravaggio among them.

Lomazzo, Giovanni Paolo

Giovanni Paolo Lomazzo (1538–1600) was one of the most important cultural figures in Lombardy during the second half of the sixteenth century. He was a painter, but is more importantly known for his treatises on art. Soon after he began studying with Giovanni Battista della Cerva in 1552, he exhibited a strong interest in the works of artists less conservative than his master. His early work is marked by the influence of Leonardo and Bernardino Luini,* as his religious frescos in the church of Santa Maria Nuova (c. 1556, Caronno, Milan) indicate. Lomazzo's writings mention that he painted several portraits during this early period, but none have been positively identified. The early 1560s brought him to Rome* where he had the opportunity of complementing his artistic education with the study of works by Michelangelo

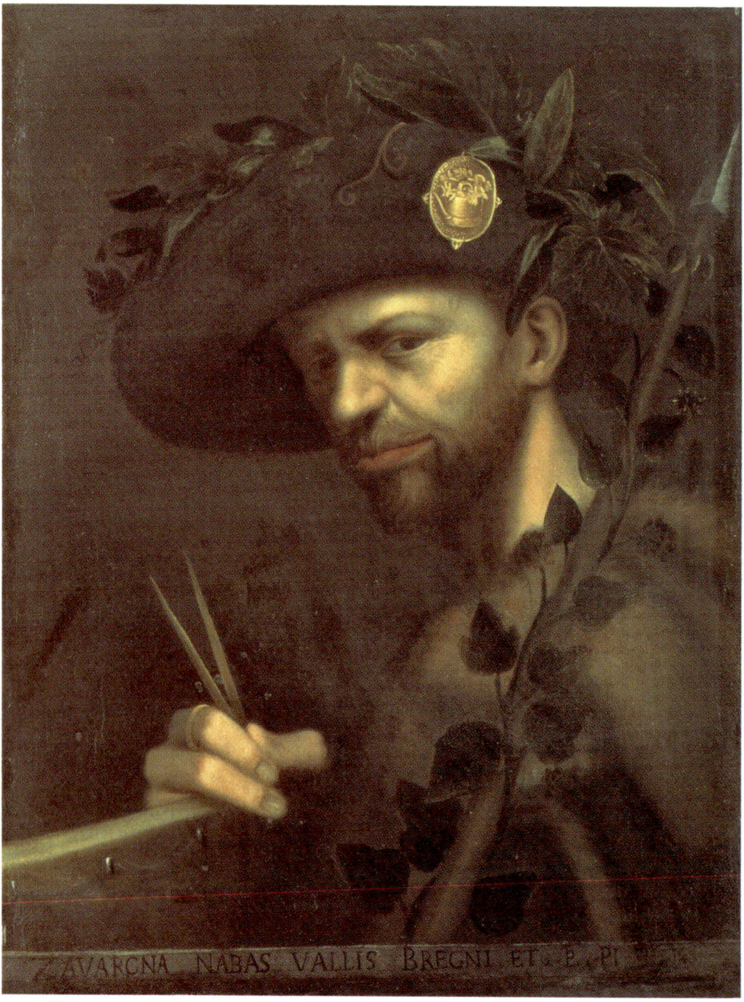

Giovanni Paolo Lomazzo, *Self-portrait.* Oil on canvas. Pinacoteca di Brera, Milan.

The man who does not restrain wantonness, allies himself with beasts. You can have no dominion greater or less than that over yourself. He who thinks little, errs much. It is easier to contend with evil at the first than at the last. No counsel is more loyal than that given on ships which are in peril: He may expect loss who acts on the advice of an inexperienced youth.

(*Codex H*, 119 [24 r.] v. Institut de France, Richter, 1192)

and the Roman-Tuscan Mannerists. A number of the works he executed upon his return to Milan,* such the *Sacrifice of Melchizedek* for the monastery of Santa Maria della Pace library, have been lost, although a *Self-portrait* dating from 1568 survives (Pinacoteca di Brera, Milan). Three years later he completed an impressive cycle of religious paintings for the Foppa Chapel of the church of San Marco, also in Milan. This is probably his best surviving artistic work. Between the end of the 1560s and the end of the 1570s he worked mainly on large altarpieces, notably a *Stigmatization of Saint Francis* (San Barnaba, Milan). After Lomazzo went blind in 1572 he devoted himself to teaching and writing on art history and theory. His works on the calculation of proportions, the rendering of emotion, the definition of chromatic values, and the treatment of chiaroscuro owe much to Leonardo's ideas and precepts. They are also an invaluable source for understanding the painting of Renaissance Lombardy.

Luini, Bernardino

Debate continues among specialists concerning Bernardino Luini's (c. 1480–1532) early life and training. The argument for his having been trained in Florence* and in Rome* during his youth is based mainly on an attribution of a copy (private collection, Venice) of Raphael's *Deposition* (Galleria Borghese, Rome). An attribution to Luini of the *Virgin and Child with Saints* (1507, Musée Jacquemart-André, Paris) signed "Bernardinus Mediolanensis" is contested by most experts. Only the *Virgin and Child Enthroned with Musician Angels* (1512, abbey of Chiaravalle, near Milan), with its manifest influence* from the illustrative techniques of the Lombard artists Vincenzo Foppa and Ambrogio Bergognone and Leonardo's *sfumato** provides a solid starting point for cataloguing his earliest works. That Luini studied Bramantino can be discerned in such paintings as *Saint Sebastian* (formerly in the Contini Bonacossi Collection, Florence), while the culmination of his architectural research is evident in the *Annunciation* (Pinacoteca di Brera, Milan). Luini probably traveled to Rome in 1515, where he may have met Leonardo and Solario,* both of whom were there at the time. It would have been then that he developed the very particular stylistic fusion of central Italian classicism and Leonardian techniques, which marked his style thereafter.

Luini owned the *Burlington House Cartoon** and apparently took inspiration from it in his version of the *Holy Family*

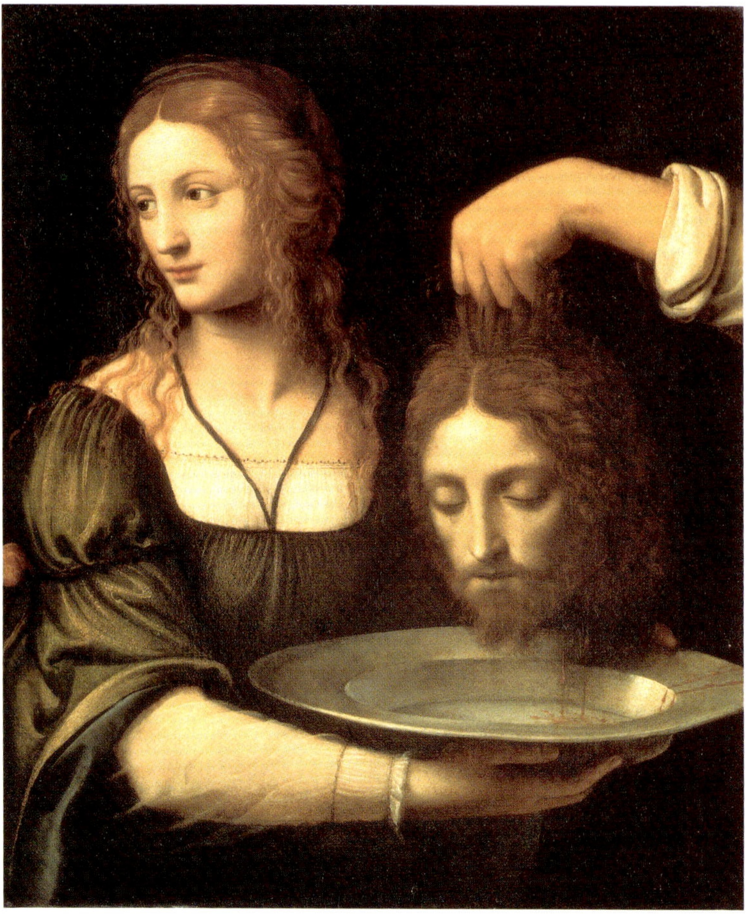

Bernardino Luini, *Salome with the Head of Saint John the Baptist.* Oil on canvas, 24 ½ × 12 ⅔ in. (62 × 55 cm). Musée du Louvre, Paris.

(Pinacoteca di Brera, Milan). He was a prolific painter, leaving behind evidence of his great narrative ease in a number of frescoes. Perhaps the finest examples are in the Besozzi Chapel (completed in 1530; church of San Maurizio, Milan). He also painted a series of *Madonnas*, a fine example of which is found in the Louvre. Nineteenth-century Romantics especially appreciated how Leonardian iconography filtered through the influence* of Solario's style. Luini's late style reached its apogee with the frescoes in the church of San Maria degli Angeli de Lugano (1529–30), where contact with German influences can be discerned.

Madonna of the Carnation

Long attributed to Verrocchio, the *Madonna of the Carnation* (Alte Pinakothek, Munich) is now almost unanimously considered a Leonardo autograph. Leonardo probably painted it some time between 1473 and 1478—although some experts think it may be his first truly autonomous work and date it to c. 1470. The original design may have been by Verrocchio*

Madonna of the Carnation, c. 1473–78. Oil on wood panel, 24 ½ × 18 ½ in. (62 × 47.5 cm). Alte Pinakothek. Munich.

but it already evidences the entire figurative repertoire of Verrocchio's best student: the Virgin's braided coiffure, the mountains viewed through haze, as theorized in the *Treatise on Painting** and also seen in the *Mona Lisa,** as well as the extremely impressive swirl of yellow fabric in the foreground, a manifestation of organic form which reappears in Leonardo's botanical and hydraulic studies. Leonardo's

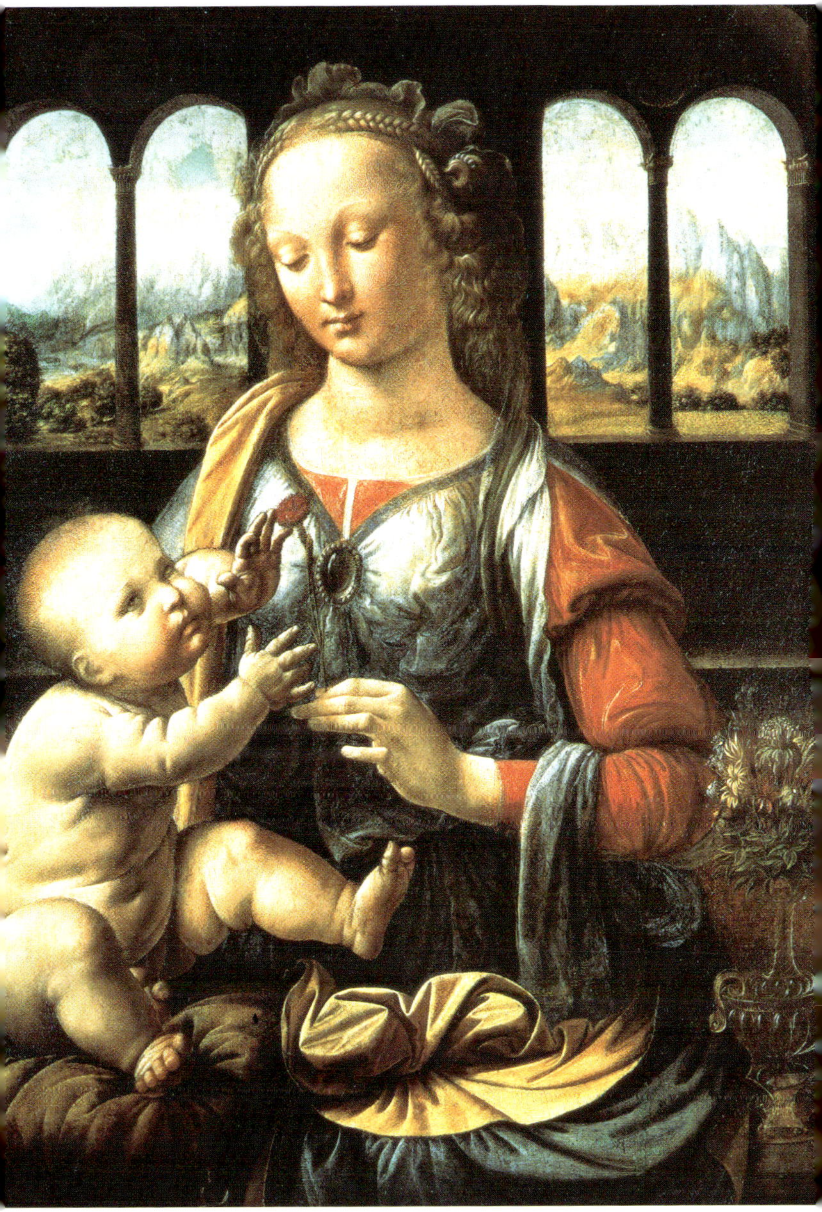

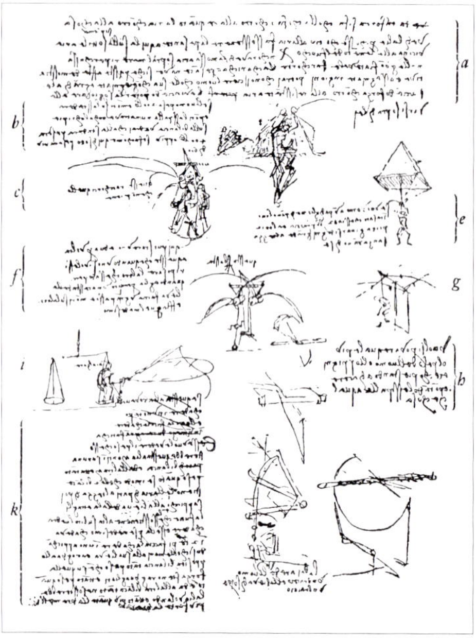

Notes for the design of parachutes and flying machines, *Codex Atlanticus*, fol. 381 v. Biblioteca Ambrosiana, Milan.

penchant for experimentation is manifest in his early use of oil paint here. It enabled him to create a translucent surface and to confer vivid highlights. The transparent vase marks his desire to be measured against the Flemish masters. Vasari* remarked this trompe l'oeil effect, which perfectly describes the piece, "a vase of water, containing some flowers, painted with a wonderful realism, which had on them dewdrops that looked more convincing than the real thing." (Bull, I, 260) But even beyond these elements, the painting introduces a new view on nature and landscape. The mountains seen through the double windows occupy three visual planes as they appear to spread out in the distance due to the conscious use of color and Leonardo's atmospheric perspective (see *Sfumato*). This is the painting's most important contribution. For here we find in a small format what will later appear in the more ambitious *Annunciation* in Florence. Judging from the number of contemporary copies that exist, the *Madonna of the Carnation* was a great success, as much in Flanders as in Italy. The Walters Art Gallery in Baltimore possesses a fine example by Ridolfo Ghirlandaio.

Manuscripts

Francesco Melzi,* Leonardo's student and friend inherited almost all of his manuscripts. He brought them to Italy, used them to compile the *Treatise on Painting** and kept them in his villa at Vaprio d'Adda near Milan until his death in 1570. His heirs had little idea of their value and thirteen pages were stolen in 1585 by the family tutor, Gavardi d'Asola. In 1588 the canon Ambrogio Mazenta convinced d'Asola to return what he had stolen, but Melzi's son Orazio was given back only seven of the original thirteen. These became the property of Pompeo Leoni, a sculptor in Madrid in the service of the Spanish king, who also acquired as many manuscripts as he could in the art markets of Milan.* He brought them to Spain with him in 1590. Upon his death his heirs offered the collection to the archduke of Tuscany who inexplicably refused it.

By 1630 several of the manuscripts had made their way to England, having been acquired by Lord Arundel. Around the same time an important grouping was purchased by Galeazzo Arconati, who donated it to the Biblioteca Ambrosiana (Milan) in 1637. Napoleon Bonaparte had these manuscripts sent to the Institut de France (Paris) in 1795, and only the *Codex*

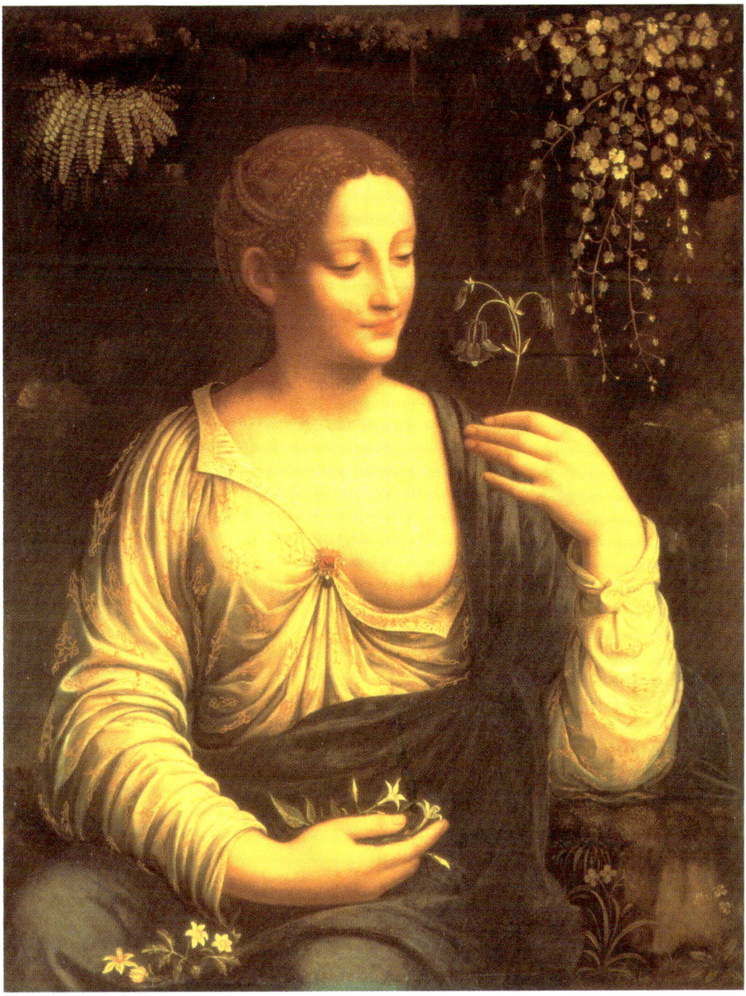

Francesco Melzi (?), *Flora*, 1520. Oil on canvas. Hermitage Museum, Saint Petersburg.

*Atlanticus** was returned to Milan under mandate of the 1815 Congress of Vienna.

In the middle of the nineteenth century a naturalized French citizen of Italian origin, Guglielmo Libri took the opportunity of an inspection of the Institut de France to steal a number of unbound pages from the collection. Libri, a renowned bibliophile and librarian who had been working for the French government, made his way to England and sold them to Lord Ashburnam. Most of the pages were subsequently lost. Still, thirteen pages were sold to Count Giacomo Manzoni in 1867; his heirs sold them to the Russian prince, Sabachnikoff, who donated them to the Italian royal family in 1893.

Only one of Leonardo's manuscripts has had a linear, traceable history, the *Leister Codex.** The present state of manuscript dispersal, between London, Madrid, Milan, Los Angeles, Paris, and Seattle, is perhaps a sort of reflection on the universal genius of their creator.

Melzi, Francesco

Francesco Melzi (c. 1491/3–c. 1500) belonged to a noble

Lombard family. He already knew Leonardo at an early age, for a letter (1508) by Leonardo exists in which he complains of not having received answers to several previous communications. Melzi's presence in Leonardo's workshop* is confirmed by a red chalk drawing* (Biblioteca Ambrosiana, Milan) of which the graphic techniques strongly resemble Leonardo's. We also have a document from 1513 in which Leonardo wrote, "left Milan* for Rome* . . . in the company of Giovan Francesco de Melsi" and three other disciples. However, Melzi was Leonardo's only student to accompany him to France* in 1517. When Leonardo wrote his last will on April 23, 1519 he named Melzi as his sole heir and executor of all his worldly goods, including the works then in his studio and all of his manuscripts.* On June 1st of that year, Melzi wrote to his brothers about his mentor's death. Melzi seems to have remained in the service of Francis I and was even named a *Familiaris* of the king and a gentleman of his court. Upon becoming the sole guardian of Leonardo's entire scientific and artistic estate, he guarded it jealously at his villa in Vaprio d'Adda. A letter dated March 6, 1523 by a military official under Duke Alfonso d'Este of Ferrara suggests that Melzi's contemporaries considered him to be the possessor of coveted Leonardo secrets. His only autograph painting, *Youth with a Parrot* (Gallarati Scotti Collection, Milan) suggests that his reputation is somewhat overrated. Stylistic similarities have led experts to attribute Melzi with a *Holy Family* (Národní Galerie, Prague) and a *Venus* (National Gallery of Art, Washington, D.C.) formerly attributed to Luini.* But other attributions, as well as a general assessment of his career as a painter, remain difficult to establish. When Vasari* visited him in 1565 he described Melzi as an affable elderly man. Upon his death, the works left to him by Leonardo were irreparably dispersed.

Milan

During the Renaissance, the duchy of Lombardy, of which Milan was the capital, was not as culturally prestigious as Tuscany, but it was one of the economically richest and most powerful military regions of the independent Italian states. For more than a century, Milan was controlled by the Visconti family, which had favored the growth of a dynamic middle class of intellectuals, merchants, and *condottieri* or professional military leaders. One of these *condottieri*, Francesco Sforza, took power in 1449. He endeavored to make the city into an artistic capital that would rival Florence* and Rome.* Among others, he called upon Tuscan architects to this end, and for the most part, they were unimpeded by existing structures in their designs for an "ideal city." The most ambitious urban project of the time was for the Castello Sforzesco, a citadel of power a short distance from the city. When Francesco Sforza

He is a poor disciple who does not excel his master.

(*Codex Forster III*, 66 v., Richter, 498)

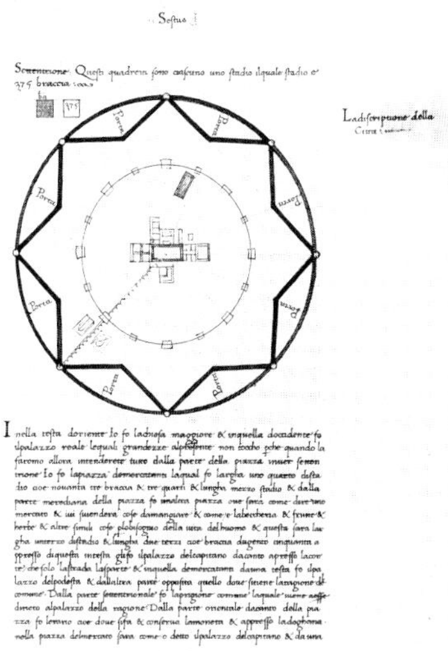

Plan for the ideal city of Sforzinda from Filarete's *Treatise on Architecture*, 1462–67. *Codex Magliabecchiano* II, fol. 43 r. Biblioteca Nazionale, Florence.

died in 1466 control went to his son, Galeazzo Maria Sforza, who was assassinated in 1476. His then seven-year-old son, Gian Galeazzo Sforza had all the authority vested in him gradually removed by his uncle, Ludovico, who ended up poisoning the boy in 1480. Lodovico then presided alone over Lombardy until 1499 and his court was one of the most sumptuous of the epoch. Artistically, late Gothic was the predominant local style, perfectly exemplified in the styles and themes employed by Bonifacio Bembo. Vincenzo Foppa was the only artist of the time who sought to assimilate the perspective of the Tuscans, while remaining within the naturalist Lombard tradition and adding in substantial doses of Flemish and Provençal influence. Bramante's* revolutionary innovations of 1474, and then Leonardo's after 1484, came up against conservative traditions still connected with the Middle Ages. But eventually their research in architecture* and sculpture* contributed to the development of distinctly classicizing tendencies. Painting's evolution was less straightforward: Bramantino brought in modern influences through a strongly personal style, while Leonardo's influence was assimilated by painters such as Giovanni Antonio Boltraffio,* Cesare da Sesto,* the de Predis* brothers, Giovanni Paolo Lomazzo, Bernardino Luini,* Francesco Melzi,* and Andrea Solario.* After the fall of the Sforza family in 1499, Francis I of France and Charles V of Spain struggled to control Milan. The latter eventually won out in 1535 and Milan remained under Spanish influence for more than a century.

MONA LISA

The presence of the *Mona Lisa*, also known as *La Gioconda* and *La Joconde*, was noted in the inventory of Leonardo's workshop* in Amboise, France in 1517 and then in Milan in 1525. It was next recorded by Cassiano dal Pozzo in 1625 as being in the French royal collection at Fontainebleau. Napoleon had it hung in his bedroom in 1800 before it was transferred to the Louvre in 1804. Its authorship has never been in doubt but the matter of its dating remains an open question. It was probably begun in 1503 or 1504 and it was certainly completed by 1513 or 1514; the rocky landscape in the background bears similarities to geological studies and drawings* dating from the latter period and suggests Leonardo's meditations on the subject of hydraulic and atmospheric action on rock. The traditional identification of the model (Mona Lisa del Giocondo), often a subject of controversy in the past, has recently been confirmed by an archival document—an accounts inventory made in 1518 by Leonardo's disciple, Salaì, which already identifies a work in his possession as the "Gioconda". Vasari* also provides a detailed description of the painting in his *Lives of the Artists*: "If one wanted to see how faithfully art can imitate nature, one could readily perceive it from this head; for here Leonardo subtly reproduced every living detail. . . . The mouth, joined to the flesh-tints of the face by the red of the lips, appeared to be living flesh rather than paint. On looking closely at the pit of her throat one could swear that pulses were beating. Altogether this picture was painted in a manner to make the most confident artist no matter who—despair and lose heart." (Bull, I, 266) Described by the French art historian André Chastel as "the illustrious misunderstood," the painting requires the effort of putting aside all the Romantic interpretations that have followed it through the centuries. For rather than being the image of a beautiful or beguiling woman, the painting is the manifestation of Leonardo's detachment from traditional conceptions of individual, psychologized portraiture in the creation of a universal model gathering together the range of his knowledge and abilities. He concentrated all his attention in rendering a three-dimensional evocation of the pulsing of blood beneath skin, and the perpetual changes undergone by beings in the natural world, such as the delicate play of contracted muscles in a mouth about to smile. Vasari's explanation is as simple as it is surprising, that Leonardo "employed singers and musicians or jesters to keep her full of merriment and so chase away the melancholy that painters usually give to portraits. As a result, in this painting of Leonardo's there was a smile so pleasing that it seemed divine rather than human." (Bull, I, 267)

Mona Lisa (*La Gioconda*), c. 1503–14. Oil on wood panel, 30 ⅓ × 20 ⅘ in. (77 × 53 cm). Musée du Louvre, Paris.

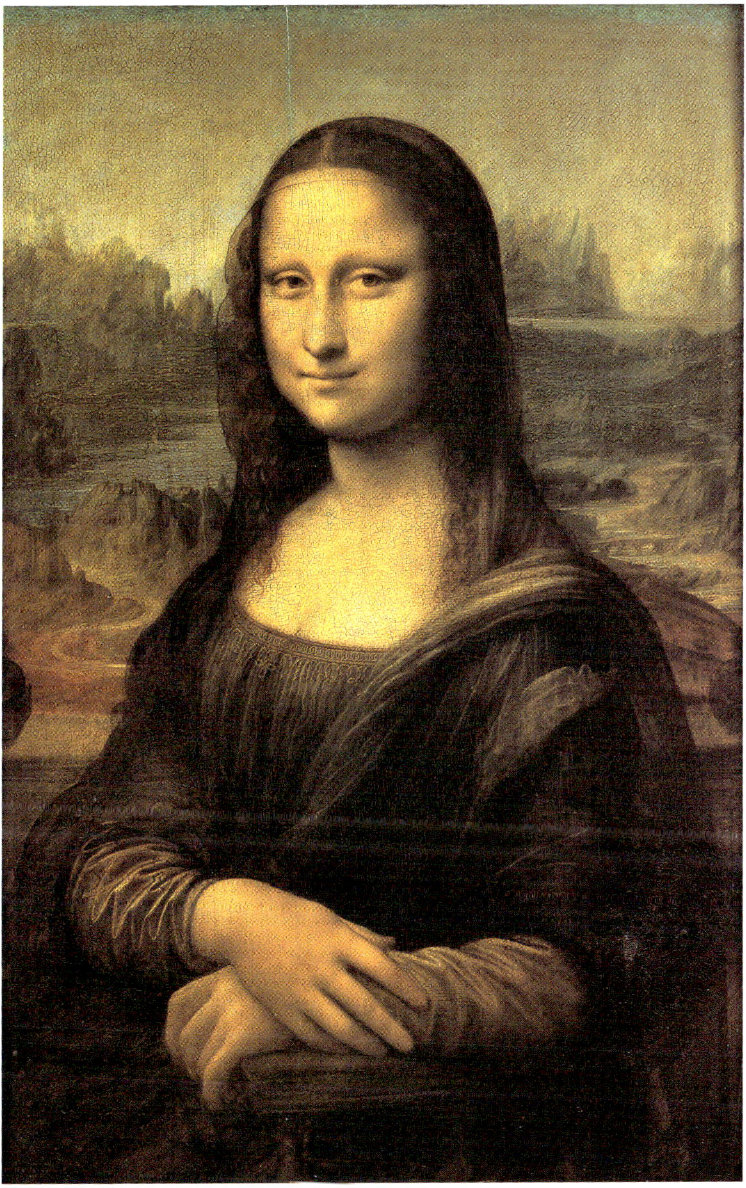

Science is the captain, and practice the soldiers.

(*Codex Atlanticus,* 76 v., Richter, 1160)

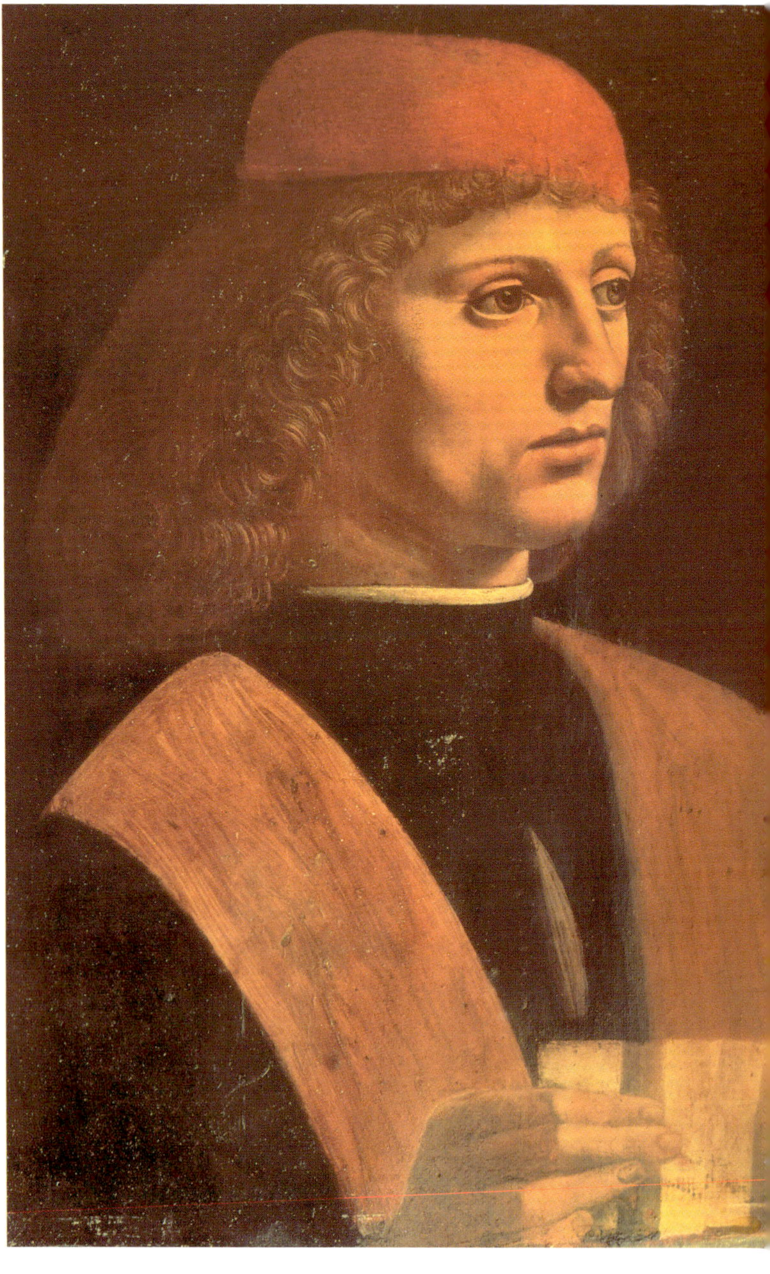

MUSICIAN, THE

After centuries of doubt and speculation, most specialists have now come to accept *The Musician* (Pinacoteca Ambrosiana, Milan) as a Leonardo autograph. They date it to 1485 on the basis of its strong stylistic affinities with the *Virgin of the Rocks.**

There are numerous hypotheses proposed concerning the identity of the sitter, including the composers Franchino Gaffurio and Josquin des Prés, both based on readings of the letters on the scroll. None have been corroborated. But the painting is apparently meant to be more of a representation of a musician as such than of a particular person. For Leonardo seems to be giving visual expression to something no painter had ever endeavored to paint—the sensation of the continued vibration of sound at the precise moment when a singer raises his eyes from his score after singing the last note of a composition. This painting effectively manifests Vasari's* claim that Leonardo gave his models movement and breath.

By the same token the painting is a manifest expression of Leonardo's perspective on the *Paragone** or debate over the supremacy of art forms. Even if he had been influenced by Antonello de Messina, in this very first portrait painted in Lombardy, Leonardo had found the way to apply his personal theory* of the "movements of the soul" and their physiological effects (see Anatomy and Physiognomy) despite the apparent stillness of the image. For this immobility actually corresponds to a barely perceptible pressure of the facial muscles and mouth. A different pigment is used on the hand and modern technical analyses have not been able to determine whether or not it was painted by Leonardo. He may have added it himself shortly after the bust was completed.

The different degrees of dilation in the pupils of the eyes have been noted and linked to this remark of Leonardo's in the *Treatise on Painting,** "This pupil in Man dilates and contracts according to the brightness or darkness of (surrounding) objects; and since it takes some time to dilate and contract, it cannot see immediately on going out of the light and into the shade, nor, in the same way, out of the shade into the light, and this very thing has already deceived me in painting an eye, and from that I learnt it." (Richter, 36. See also *Sfumato.*)

The Musician, c. 1465. Oil on wood panel, 17 × 12 ¼ in. (43 × 31 cm). Pinacoteca Ambrosiana, Milan.

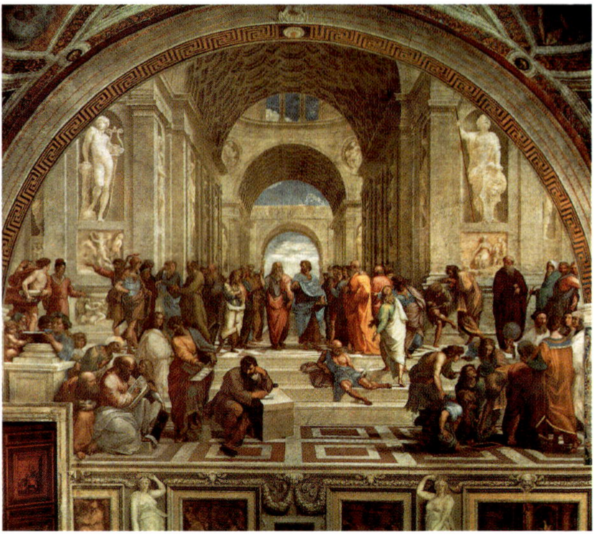

Raphael, *The School of Athens*, 1509–10. Fresco. Vatican, Stanza della Segnatura.

Neoplatonism

Because his approach to everything was so pragmatic, Leonardo had less use for preestablished systems of thought than many of his contemporaries. His extremely keen and alert mind led him to a great mistrust of "false sciences" and even, to a certain extent, of theology. Still, on the one hand, his scientific perspective cannot be compared, for instance, to that of Descartes a century and a half later. And on the other, his search for underlying relations among all things likens his position to that of neoplatonism. This movement was born in Florence, * and its development was directly related to the city's Platonic Academy which formed around the philosopher Marsilio Ficino (1433–99). Its members were impassioned readers of Plato's dialogues and Leonardo must have come into some contact with them in his youth, despite the fact that he did not know Greek or Latin at the time. Ficino conceived of the universe as a great chain of being comprised of four hierarchized elements: the universal mind, a purely intellectual and super-celestial domain; the world soul which is indestructible but not immutable; nature which is composed of the combinations and disjoinings of form and matter; and the inert and lifeless world of matter. Just as the world is divided between material and immaterial domains, man is composed of a body and a soul with the latter comprised of two parts, the *anima prima* and the *anima secunda*. Animals are supplied with *anima secunda*. But through spiritual ascetism, *anima prima* has the capacity of reaching rational truths and the practicing of the highest possible art, direct contemplation of God. Humans therefore occupy a unique place on earth and can attain temporal happiness before their death in two ways, through the *via activa* or the *via contempletiva*, both of which guarantee Redemption in the hereafter. Although his perspective takes a different

PAINTER'S STATUS

For Leonardo a painter's education had to consist in more than a series of exercises leading to technical mastery. It had to reach the point of being a form of asceticism, liberating the mind from the traps of subjectivity and simplicity. "The youth should first learn perspective, then the proportions of objects. Then he may copy from some good master, to accustom himself to fine forms. Then from nature, to confirm by practice the rules he has learnt. Then see for a time the works of various masters. Then get the habit of putting his art into practice and work." (*Codex A*, Institut de France, 97 v., Richter, 483) The dignity of the artist was an absolute for Leonardo. His exceptional intelligence, the magnitude and depth of his scientific research, and his conception of painting as a *cose mentale* (see *Paragone*), led him to unequivocally condemn more artisanal painting, in which habitual methods are more or less adept manifestations of currently popular themes and set patterns. For Leonardo, it was the painter's duty to be continually self critical and to eschew any sort of complacency. "To the end that well-being of the body may not injure that of the mind, the painter or draughtsman must remain solitary, and particularly when intent on those studies and reflections which will constantly rise up before his eye, giving materials to be well stored in the memory. While you are alone you are entirely your own [master] and if you have one companion you are but half your own, and the less so in proportion to the indiscretion of his behaviour. And if you have many companions you will fall deeper into the same Trouble." (*Codex A*, Institut de France, 97 v., Richter, 494) Leonardo believed that painting encompassed all sorts of activities, including moral and religious ones. Several angry notes denouncing "hypocrites" seem to be slightly veiled expressions of his aversion to the austerity imposed upon artists in Florence* under the Savanarola government at the end of the fifteenth century.

form than that of the neoplatonists, he also sees analogies between the human organism and the structure of the world (see Beauty). But the growing pessimism of his later years, as the drawings of *A Deluge* (Windsor Castle, Royal Library) suggest, led him to a view of the world where the forces of nature would eventually eliminate every trace of human activity.

Paragone

During the Renaissance, arguments over which of the arts was superior to the others were quite common and known as the *Paragone*. Leonardo contributed his own particular version, but for him it was more than a petty controversy or a stylistic exercise. Leonardo's consideration of painting as the highest expression of the mind was an essential aspect of all his activity. First of all, as opposed to Scholastic thinking, he believed that knowledge had to be based in experience; he gave experience form and body through drawing* and the elaboration of mechanical models. Second, in an effort to prove the superiority of visual over temporal arts, he opposed those which require a succession of signs (literature and music) to those whose signs are present all at once (sculpture,* and painting,* but not architecture* due to its being too mechanical). The visual arts could offer a full and synthesized perception of nature, but the temporal arts were only analytic and constituent. Lastly, he gauged the

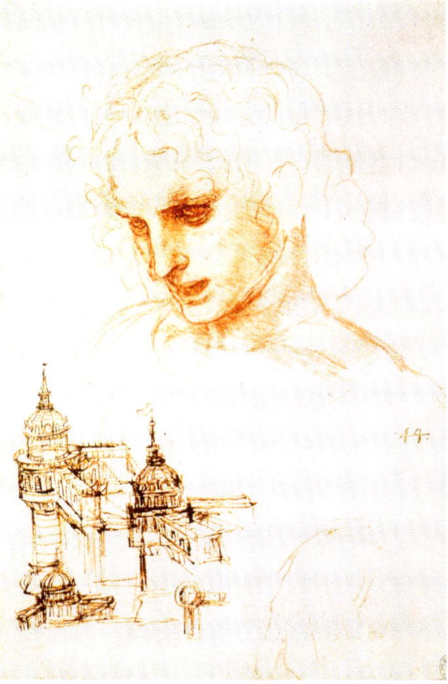

Angel and architectural study for the *Last Supper, Codex Windsor.* Red chalk and pen on white paper. Windsor Castle, Royal Library.

relative capacities and merits of painting versus sculpture. Both these arts of representation engage all the powers of the visual world in a condensed form. But sculpture has neither the power of light nor of illusion that Leonardo sought to demonstrate in all his paintings. For example, the visual and sculptural grouping of figures he learned from Verrocchio* effectively proved to him that the third dimension is at least as present in painting as it is in sculpture. Finally, he came to consider that painting is an intellectual and not a manual activity. Quattrocento artists and their humanist spokesmen had already prepared the way for a perspective on painting as a *cosa mentale*, a thing of the mind occupying the summit of the structure of knowledge by its total synthesis of mental and physical reality.

Patrons

Leonardo arrived in Florence* in 1466 to enter Verrocchio's* workshop.* In 1472, at about age twenty, he was registered at the Saint Luke's painters' guild. His first known commission was for the priors of the Signoria for an altarpiece in the chapel of San Bernardo in the Palazzo Vecchio. Leonardo replaced Piero Pollaiuolo on the project and was paid 25 florins. He began work on the altarpiece but he too was eventually replaced by Ghirlandaio and then by Filippino Lippi. His second recorded commission was from the monks of the San Donato at Scopeto for the *Adoration of the Magi**in 1481. But Leonardo turned out to be most productive when he worked directly in the court of a patron, and about a year later he went into the service of the court of Ludovico Sforza in Milan.* He stayed attached to Ludovico's court for sixteen years during which time he wrote the *Treatise on Painting** and worked on the equestrian monument to Ludovico's father, Francesco Sforza (see Sculpture), which was never realized in his time. His first project in Milan was a commission for the Confraternità dell' Immacolata Concezione in their chapel in San Francesco Grande that he and the Predis* brothers (see *Virgin of the Rocks*) were commissioned to do. He also painted *Lady with an Ermine* (Czartoryski Muzeum, Krakow) and the *Last Supper** and worked on his first notebook, the *Codex Trivulziano.** With the fall of Ludovico in 1499, Leonardo traveled briefly and then returned to Florence the following year. In 1502 he became Cesare Borgia's military engineer and in 1503 he apparently worked with Niccolò Machiavelli on a project to divert the Arno River away from Pisa, Florence's foe. It was during this period that he painted the *Mona Lisa** and worked on the public commission, the *Battle of Anghiari* fresco (see Introduction). In 1506 he returned to Milan and entered the service of Charles d'Amboise, the French governor of the city. This was the period of the second *Virgin of the Rocks,* the painting of *Saint John the Baptist,** and the planning for another unrealized equestrian monument, this time to General Gian Giacomo Trivulzio, and made tremendous progress in his research in fluid dynamics, geometry, and anatomical drawing.* Leonardo became involved with Giuliano de' Medici, duke of Nemours and his brother the Medici Pope Leo X in Rome in 1513. He probably worked on military projects for the Medici, traveled some with Giuliano and worked avidly on his researches in geometry, optics, and anatomy. Giuliano died in 1515 and it is most likely around this time that he met Francis I when the new French king was in Bologna meeting Leo X. Francis invited Leonardo to France.* The artist arrived there in 1516 or 1517 and he continued his research, finished some paintings, worked on court entertainments* and was a very sought-after figure. Leonardo died on May 2, 1519 in Cloux, near Amboise.

Personality

Accounts of Leonardo by those who knew him all describe how appealing he was to his contemporaries and the care he took when he appeared in public. Both of these features apparently explain why he was so popular at the most prestigious courts of his day. However, we should not forget that counterbalancing his cultivation and politeness was a continual involvement in the design of deadly war machines, of which the violence evidently fascinated him. His multifaceted and even paradoxical personality enabled him to follow his scientific curiosity into dispassionate explorations of all aspects of anatomy* and psychology while having a certain disdain of physiological activity and human foibles. Secretiveness seems to have been one of his primary personality traits, and effectively functioned to protect his inventions by rendering them incomprehensible to anyone other than himself. His handwriting, for example, could only be read when held up to a mirror and reversed. It is impossible to say to what extent he invented his own personality. If he did, was his model the wise sorcerer, the philosopher with the keys to universal knowledge celebrated by the neoplatonists* in the figure of Hermes? No definitive portrait of Leonardo exists. People have often sought to recognize him in the features of figures in his works, or in the works of his contemporaries. Examples include Verrocchio's* *David* (Museo del Bargello, Florence) or *The School of Athens* by Raphael (Musei Vaticani, Rome), but these have never been confirmed. The same holds true for the famous red chalk drawing said to be a self-portrait (Biblioteca Reale, Turin,); there is no evidence that the traditional identification of the model is correct. His manuscripts reveal an extraordinary capacity for self-analysis and self-splitting. He often develops his theories* by using a dialogue with an imagined adversary he

Self-Portrait (?), c. 1512. Red chalk, 13 × 8 ⅓ in. (33.3 × 21.3 cm) Biblioteca Reale, Turin.

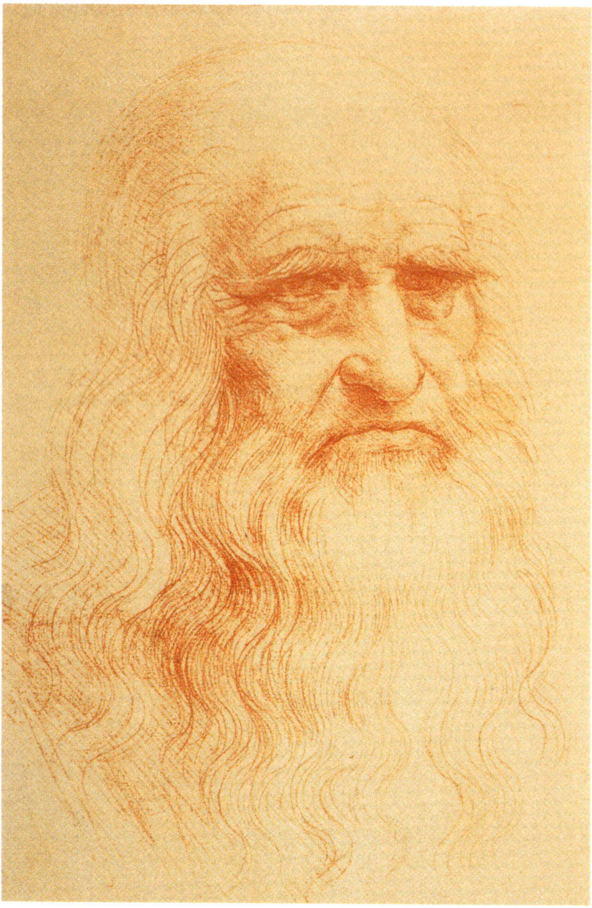

must convince (see Criticism). The biographical indications he left in his notebooks most often concern only a great variety of practical details, and do not provide any personal information, or do so only obliquely. The most surprising account he provides is certainly the following, "I've squandered my time." (Windsor Library, fol. 12 v.)

Portrait of Isabella d'Este

Although previously attributed to Giovanni Antonio Boltraffio,* the *Portrait of Isabella d'Este* (Musée du Louvre, Graphic arts department, Paris) is now almost unanimously attributed to Leonardo and thought to have been executed between the end of 1499 and the beginning of 1500 during a trip to Mantua. In a letter to Isabella d'Este, Cecilia Gallerani (the subject of the *Lady with an Ermine*) recommends Leonardo as one of the most gifted portraitists of the time, and the most capable of creating the likeness of the famous Marchesa of Mantua. For a long time, the pastel in the Louvre attracted little art historical or critical attention. This was probably due to its poor condition caused by inappropriate conservation, and it's profile view (the only example by Leonardo) which owes so much to a medallion made by Gian Cristoforo Romano in 1498. But these are not very good reasons for neglect! Consider, for example, the way in which the model authoritatively dominates the foreground with her shoulders seeming to turn slowly into a three-quarter view. The face however is surprisingly uninspired. We know that Isabella did not like sitting for long periods with her artists, and so Leonardo probably worked directly from Romano's image. Still, it must be said that the style he had been developing progressively in the portraits of his first Lombard period are given fully satisfying expression here, and that this style would go on to be tremendously popular in Venice.* In a letter dated March 13, 1500 the great instrument maker Lorenzo Gusnasco da Pavia compares this portrait to those of Giovanni Bellini, and finds those of the latter more stiff. And Giorgione learned much from the inventions of Leonardo (his senior by twenty-five years), putting them to use to renew and intensify the iconographic techniques of Venetian portraiture.

Predis, de (Brothers)

The artist Giovanni Ambrogio (c. 1455–c. 1508) was the youngest of the de Predis (or Preda) brothers and probably learned the art of miniature illuminating from his half-brother Cristoforo (c. 1440–c. 1486). In 1479 he was named to the Milanese* mint (the Zecca), where he worked with another of his brothers, Bernardino, and in 1482 he was working at the court of Ludovico Sforza. He met Leonardo the next year and collaborated with him on an altarpiece commissioned by the Confraternità dell'Immacolata Concezione for the San Francesco Grande Chapel (see the *Virgin of the Rocks*); he painted the two music-making angel side panels now in London's National Gallery. Cristoforo was active in the Sforza court, where he produced many portraits, including a charcoal drawing of *Bianca Maria Sforza.* When Bianca married Emperor Maximilian I, Giovanni Ambrogio went to Germany with her. In 1495 Maximilian entrusted him, along with Francesco Galli and Accino da Lecco with the fabrication of his new coins, and then, in July of the same year he returned to Milan. In 1498 he received new portrait commissions, notably one of *Emperor Maximilian* (Kunsthistorisches Museum, Vienna). He was intensely active in several domains. Working for both the Milanese and Imperial courts, he designed ceremonial fabrics and clothing, stage scenery, and supervised the weaving of tapestries. But it was as a portraitist that his patrons most appreciated him. Finally, a few religious

Portrait of Isabella d'Este, c. 1499–1500. Black chalk with charcoal and pastel on paper, 24 7/8 × 18 1/8 in. (63 × 46 cm). Musée du Louvre, Graphic arts department, Paris.

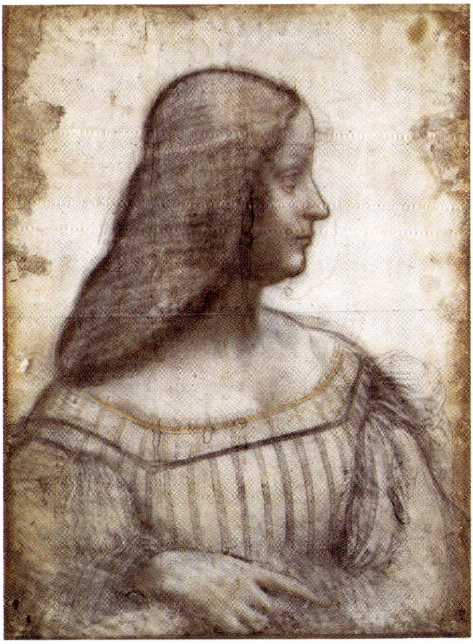

paintings which evidence the influence* of Leonardo must be mentioned. In some cases, Giovanni Ambrogio explicitly made use of Leonardo's drawings* and compositions, as in the *Litta Madonna* (Hermitage Museum, Saint Petersburg).
Evangelista (c. 1445–90), another half-brother is less well known. He lived in a house in Milan near the Porta Ticinese, where Leonardo probably stayed when he first arrived in that city. This suggests that da Vinci was socially as well as professionally involved with the de Predis brothers. The sole mention of Evangelista in archival documents cites his collaboration on the Confraternità dell'Immacolata Concezione project mentioned above. His participation was probably limited to gilding and some trompe l'oeil figures (National Gallery, London). That is practically all that is known of his artistic output.

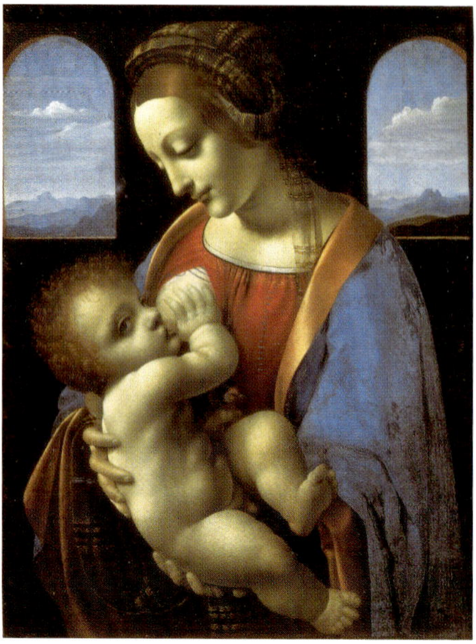

Giovanni Ambrogio de Predis, *Madonna and Child* (*Litta Madonna*), c. 1490. Oil on wood panel, 16 ½ × 12 ⅞ in. (42 × 33 cm). Hermitage Museum, Saint Petersburg.

Prophecies

"Of Money and Gold: Out of cavernous pits a thing shall come forth which will make all the nations of the world toil and sweat with the greatest torments, anxiety and labour, that they may gain its aid." (*Codex Atlanticus,* 37 v., Richter, 1328)
"Of Dreaming: Men will seem to see new destructions in the sky. The flames that fall from it will seem to rise in it and to fly from it with terror. They will hear every kind of animals speak in human language. They will instantaneously run in person in various parts of the world, without motion. They will see the greatest splendour in the midst of darkness. O! marvel of the human race! What madness has led you thus! You will speak with animals of every species and they with you in human speech. You will see yourself fall from great heights without any harm and torrents will accompany you, and will mingle with their rapid course. (*Codex Atlanticus,* 37 v., Richter, 1298)
"Of Ants: These creatures will form many communities, which will hide themselves and their young ones and victuals in dark caverns, and they will feed themselves and their families in dark places for many months without any light, artificial or natural." (*Codex Atlanticus,* 37 v., Richter, 1293)
"Of Sawyers: There will be many men who will move one against another, holding in their hands a cutting tool. But these will not do each other any injury beyond tiring each other; for, when one pushes forward the

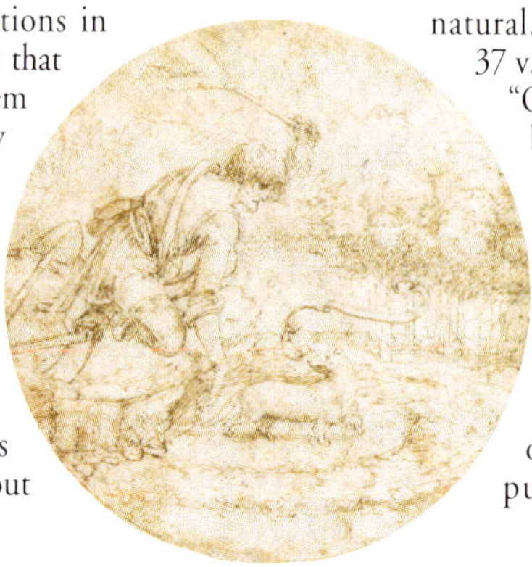

other will draw back. But woe to him who comes between them! For he will end by being cut in pieces. (*Codex Atlanticus,* 370 r., Richter, 1295)

"Of a Man's Shadow which moves with him: Shapes and figures of men and animals will be seen following these animals and men wherever they flee. And exactly as the one moves the other moves; but what seems so wonderful is the variety of height they assume. (ibid.)

"Of Constellations: And many creatures of land and water will go up among the stars (that is Planets)." (*Codex Atlanticus,* 370 r., Richter, 1304)

"The bones of the Dead will be seen to govern the fortunes of him who moves them (By Dice)." (*Codex Atlanticus,* 370 r., Richter, 1031)

"Of the Dead which are carried to be buried: The simple folks will carry vast quantities of lights to light up the road for those who have entirely lost the power of sight." (*Codex Atlanticus,* 370 r., Richter, 1296)

Rome

Rome's status as premier political and artistic city increased during Leonardo's day. In the fifteenth century, serious architectural projects and paintings were deferred due to the brevity of papal reigns and the popes' difficulties in imposing authority. Even if Nicolas V (1447–55) and Sixtus IV (1471–84) resolutely endeavored to restore Rome's former greatness, the city still had no local artistic establishment that could rival Florence's.* This explains why Tuscan and Umbrian painters were called upon in the first stages of the decoration of the Sistine Chapel. Meanwhile, thanks to its ruins, the city offered an endless repertoire of motifs, which excited the imagination of almost every artist who went there. Things changed however under Pope Julius II (1503–13). His ascendancy was not only marked by an ideological program aimed at reaffirming the spiritual and temporal power of the papacy, it also led to an actualization of the humanist ideal of synthesizing the greatness of ancient Rome with Christian Rome through the architectural, sculptural, and painted works of Bramante,* Michelangelo, and Raphael. Leonardo does not seem to have influenced local Roman artistic production very much. (At least there is nothing comparable to his influence in Milan* and Lombardy). His stay in Rome was short but put him in direct contact with the ancient sculptures, traces of which often appear in his later paintings. Under Pope Leo X (1513–22) it was unarguably Raphael and not Leonardo who produced the most fascinating religious tableaus. Raphael was given almost all public and private commissions and was put in charge of nearly all works done under the auspices of the papacy. When Charles V sacked the city in 1527 most of the artists still residing there fled to other Italian or European courts. Leonardo had provided an example with his departure for France.* A number of more or less cryptic annotations in his notebooks suggest that he had foreseen the undoing of the papal state.

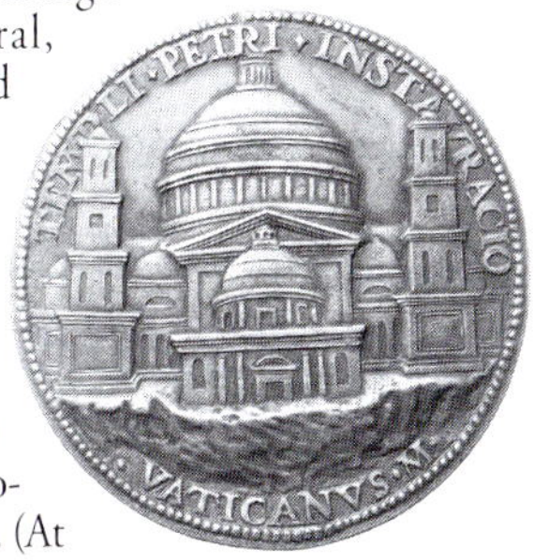

Caradosso, early design of Saint Peter's Basilica medal, 1503.

Facing page: *The Ermine, Symbol of Purity,* c. 1494. Pen and ink over traces of black chalk on paper. Fitzwilliam Museum, Cambridge, England.

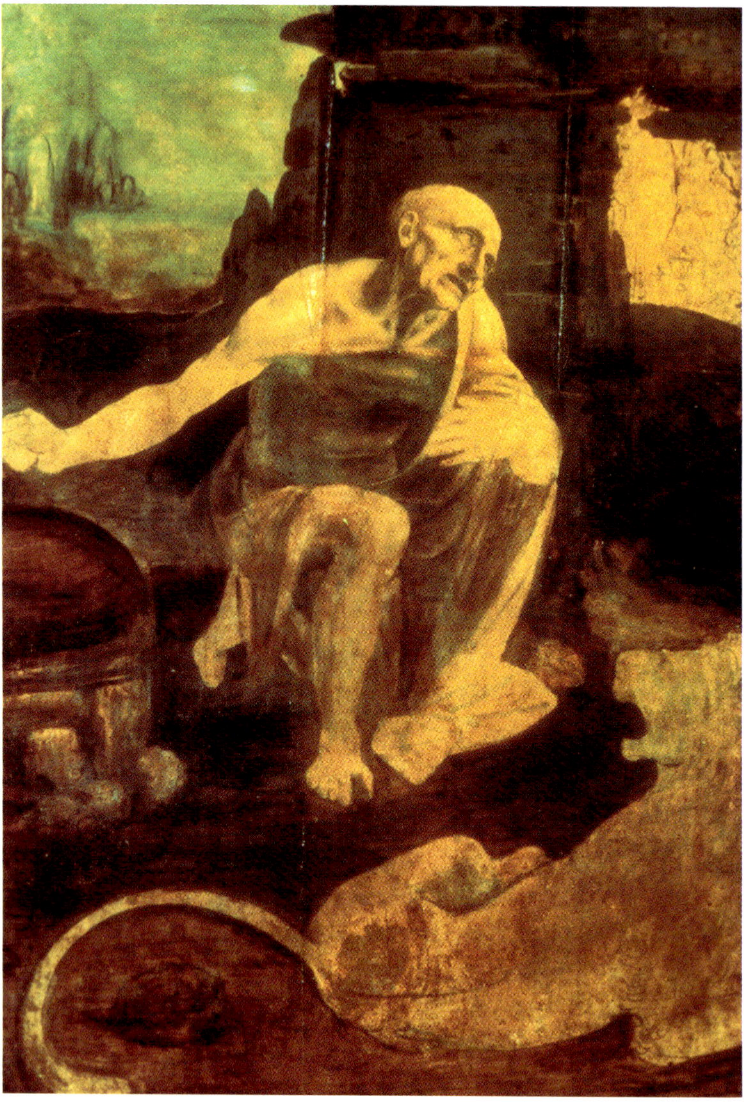

Saint Jerome, 1480.
Tempera and oil on wood panel,
3 ft. 4 ½ × 2 ft. 5 ½ in. (103 × 75 cm).
Musei Vaticani, Rome.

SAINT JEROME

There has never been any doubt that *Saint Jerome* (Vatican, Pinacoteca) is by the hand of Leonardo. Leonardo's disciple Salaì inherited the painting, and in 1525 it was still in Milan.* Experts date it to about 1480. It is the fruit of long study of human anatomy* and human proportions put to the service of purely artistic ends in a renewed effort by Leonardo to master the representation of three dimensions on a flat surface. The crouching saint's position recalls ancient sculpture, while his outstretched arm measures the space about him and his downward projecting legs anticipate Leonardo's famous *Vitruvian Man* (Galleria dell'Accademia, Venice). Jerome's ascetically fleshless body also seems to be a direct response to Leonardo's regular dissections, a practice he maintained to learn as much as possible about the structure of bones and muscles. While the image has its basis in works of classical antiquity, it also effectively translates several sculptures, produced in Verrocchio's* studio, into painting, notably the two statue portraits of old men now in the Victoria and Albert Museum, London. Vasari* laments a lost head of Saint Jerome which was held to be marvelous and sculpted by Verrocchio himself.

The painting's unfinished state reveals a good deal about how it was made. The landscape in the left background is defined in long thick painted brushstrokes on which the painter's fingerprints can be made out, evidence that even at this early point in his career, Leonardo was already experimenting in this way with hazy *sfumato* effects. The church on the right, the saint, and the lion at his feet were all sketched with a brush. White highlights are applied over the yellowish browns, for example on the right leg and neck, to express anatomical relief. The beauty and savage energy of the lion are the result of its half heraldic, half naturalistic rendering, which along with the turn of the animal's head and open jaws confirm Leonardo's ambivalence and fascination with the world of wild untamed instinct.

This painting inaugurates a new phase in Leonardo's career. From now on his subjects are usually treated dramatically, which is quite suggestive of the neoplatonic* viewpoint of cultured Florentine circles on the place of mankind in the universe and their search for transcendence.

SAINT JOHN THE BAPTIST

Saint John the Baptist (Musée du Louvre) was most probably painted for Giovanni Benci and it is mentioned as being present in Leonardo's studio* in Amboise in 1517. It is generally thought to have been done towards the end of the second period in Florence.* While it's attribution has never been questioned, the painting has not been received with unconditional admiration by modern art historians, some of whom are troubled by the unusual mocking expression on this ascetic prophet (whose traditional attributes are a cruciform staff and animal skin) who preached penitence and announced the coming of the messiah. *Saint Jerome** is the only other example of a religious painting by Leonardo with only a single figure. But in that case the landscape and the lion play essential compositional roles. Here the saint is completely isolated and looks directly and insistently at the viewer. Formally *Saint John the Baptist* is one of the artist's most striking efforts to suggest relief with the use of chiaroscuro alone and not depending on mathematical perspective. As he often repeats in his manuscripts,* he considered relief the product of a an optical relationship between an object and the ground surrounding it. In this case, the image itself has darkened over time, so assessing the success of the project is difficult. But in the better preserved sections all the subtlety of the changes in tonalities can be discerned in the progressive transitions from light to dark zones, as well as the different nuances of reflected light on the hair, the animal skin, and the flesh tones. To paraphrase Edouard Manet, one might say that light is the main character in this painting and it plays the double role of physical illumination and symbolic manifestation of divine transcendence. The light that certain elements give off through the shadow has been related to Leonardo's scientific research on the *lumen cinereum* of the moon. In addition, the stylistic rendering of the soft curling hair is identical to that in Leonardo's studies of vortices and whirlpools. As Leonardo himself explained, "Observe the motion of the surface of the water, which resembles that of hair, and has two motions, of which one goes on with the flow of the surface, the other forms the lines of the eddies." (Windsor Castle, Royal Library, f. 12579 r., Richter, 389)

Every thing proceeds from every thing, and every thing becomes every thing, and every thing can be turned into every thing else, because that which exists in the elements is composed of those elements.

(*Codex Atlanticus*, 385 v., Richter, 1473)

Saint John the Baptist, c. 1513–16. Oil on wood panel, 27 ⅕ x 22 ½ in. (69 x 57 cm). Musée du Louvre, Paris.

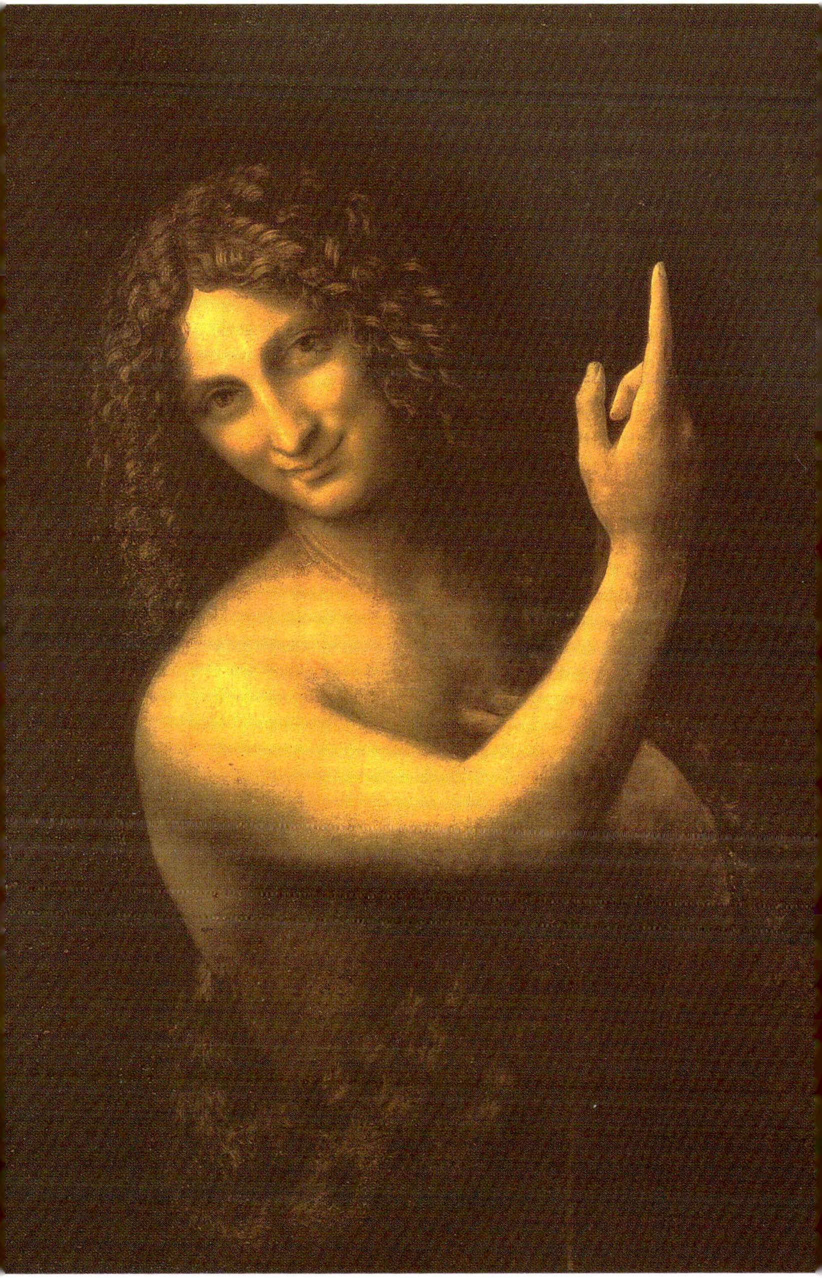

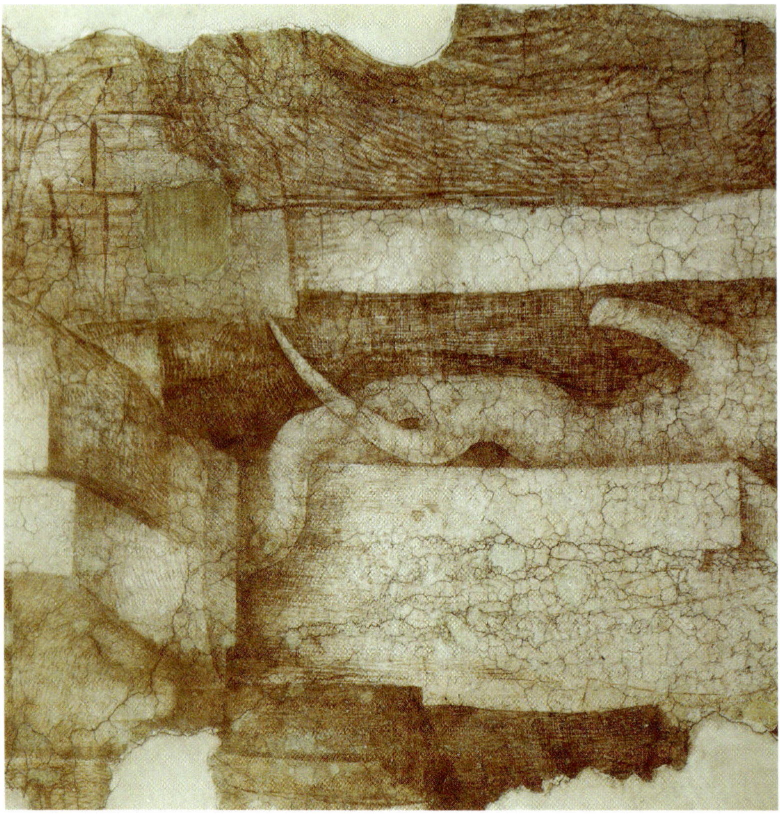

Roots and rocks (detail from the northeast wall), c. 1487–89. Fresco. Castello Sforzesco, Sala delle Asse, Milan.

Sala delle Asse

All that remains of Leonardo's decoration of the Sala delle Asse (chamber of pikes) in the Castello Sforzesco in Milan are the great intertwining tree and rope motifs that rise up the walls to the ceiling. These were first rediscovered towards the end of the nineteenth century but left beneath layers of paint and plaster because it was thought they were not Leonardo's original work. Upon their second rediscovery in 1954 critical opinion unanimously declared them to be Leonardo autographs and dated them to between 1487 and 1498. Leonardo's love of labyrinthine interweavings of natural motifs finds superb expression here. To the extent that the fragmentary nature of the work allows speculation, the intertwining vegetation was conceived according to a very sophisticated layered and architectonic design. The blue of the sky can be discerned between the interstices of the branches, giving the impression of an open wall above and behind. Roots winding among rocky layers and spreading up into a great tree trunk are painted onto a large section of wall. All this suggests that Leonardo decorated the entire chamber with unified trompe-l'oeil murals including vegetation that seemed to grow up out of the ground to overwhelm architectural details. Here again, Leonardo's fascination with the opposition between organic natural growth and architectural solidity marries his capacities for using analytic and experimental means to arrive at the greatest possible expressiveness. These mural paintings are much more than simple evidence of virtuosity in illusionistic techniques. They suggest an intense battle between the stability of the mineral and the vitality of the vegetable worlds within an image resulting from a precarious balance among opposing forces. The *Sala delle Asse* gives the impression of a continually metamorphosing landscape. It presents a view of the world only Leonardo's painting is capable of rendering, where every element continually acts against the others.

Scapiliata, La

The head of a young woman known as *La Scapiliata* (Pinacoteca Nazionale, Parma) has only recently been accepted by specialists as the work of Leonardo and recognized as the "young tousle haired woman, a sketch by Leonardo da Vinci," mentioned in the 1627 inventory of the Gonzaga Collection in Mantua. Dating the work, however, is still difficult; perhaps it was painted in Leonardo's early days in Florence.* There are technical and stylistic similarities to other unfinished works from that period, such as the *Adoration of the Magi** and *Saint Jerome.** It could be the sketch for a woman's portrait like those

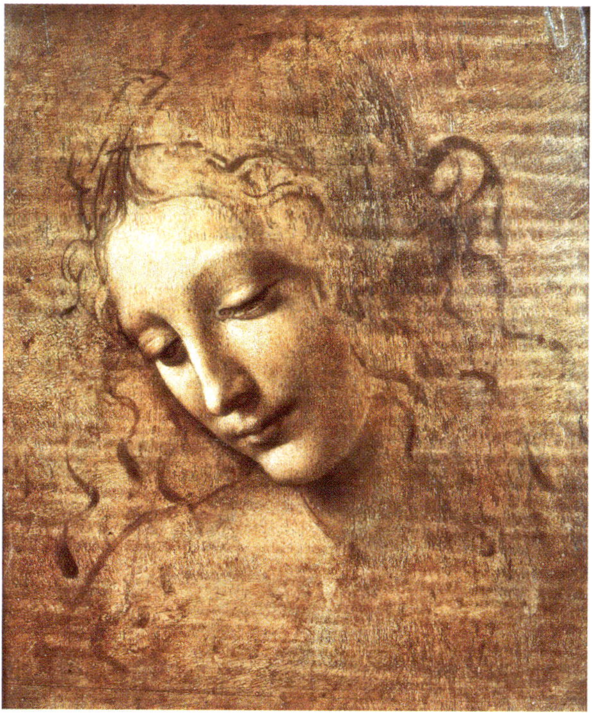

La Scapiliata, c. 1508. Mixed media on wood panel, 9 ½ × 8 ¼ in. (24.6 × 21 cm). Pinacoteca Nazionale, Parma.

from the early Lombard period. Or it might be a later work from around 1508. At that point Leonardo was returning to themes and techniques he had employed earlier on, but transforming them into a style where volumes emerge emphatically from the picture surface—as is the case for the beautiful oval face. Experts consider the last hypothesis the most probable. The unfinished nature of *La Scapiliata* reveals a technique that differs somewhat from Leonordo's typical practices, for the young woman's head was drawn directly onto unprepared wood with a brush and then heightened with white. This is the sole example of an apparently improvised painting by Leonardo. Much of its appeal derives from the impression of spontaneity it evokes. Many commentators have remarked the subtlety in the rendering of contour and flesh tones with such a simple chromatic range: black, white, and beige.

Study of a horse. Metal point on paper. Musée Bonnat, Bayonne.

SCULPTURE

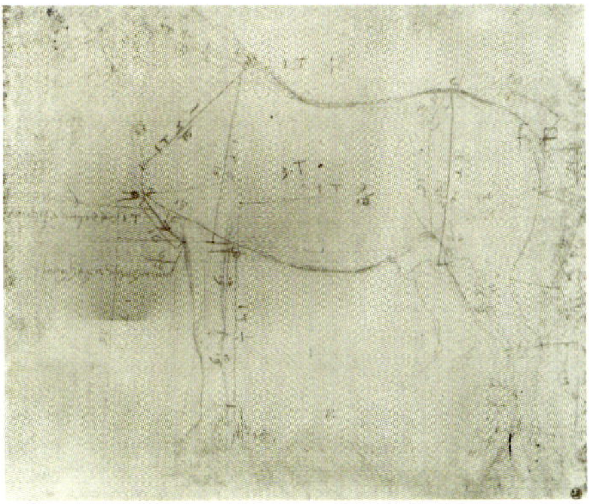

There is no doubt that Leonardo practiced as a sculptor, but to date it has been nearly impossible to attribute specific works to him. His most famous sculptural project is the great equestrian monument to Francesco Sforza, commissioned by his son Ludovico. Anonimo Gaddiano* explains, "In Milan* he made an enormous horse with duke Francesco Sforza astride it; a beautiful work to be cast in bronze. But everyone judged it to be impossible, insisting particularly that it could never be cast as a single piece, so the work was never executed." (See *Codex Madrid.*) Five hundred years later, through the efforts of Charles Dent and the Tallix Foundry in the state of New York, Leonardo's notations were followed to create the Sforza horse. Although it was cast in seven pieces these have now been attached and the statue has been placed in front of the Milan horse track. We know Leonardo's plans for another equestrian monument to Gian Giacomo Trivulzio from a series of pen drawings* (Windsor Castle, Royal Library). These show a spirited horse above a very elaborate base. The closest thing to real material evidence of Leonardo's sculptural talents are according to Vasari,* a group of "three bronze figures over the north door of San Giovanni [in Florence*] which were executed by Giovanfrancesco Rustici, under Leonardo's direction, and which as far as design and finish are concerned are the finest casts yet seen in modern times." (Bull, I, 271) It is also highly probable that Leonardo sculpted small clay or wax pieces. Specialists have long been in search of any surviving examples, or of their bronze castings. A shortsighted examination, based on the dearth of surviving evidence, might lead one to conclude that Leonardo's impact on sculpture was not great, but he did influence his contemporaries. Thus, in praise of the artist's sculptural production, Vasari concluded: "Because of Leonardo we have a deeper knowledge of human anatomy and the anatomy of the horse." (ibid.)

Solario, Andrea

Andrea Solario (c. 1465–1524) came from an influential family of architects and sculptors. From 1481 to 1492 he worked with his brothers in the family workshop* in Milan.*

In the early 1490s he spent time in Venice* where he painted a graceful *Virgin and Child with Saints,* his earliest known work (Museo Poldi Pezzoli, Milan), as well as an interesting *Virgin with Carnations* (Pinacoteca di Brera, Milan), and a fascinating *Virgin and Child with Saints Simon and Joseph* (Pinacoteca di Brera, Milan), a variation on the typical Venetian theme of the "sacred conversation."

Solario was back in Milan sometime after 1495, and in 1500 he bought property there.

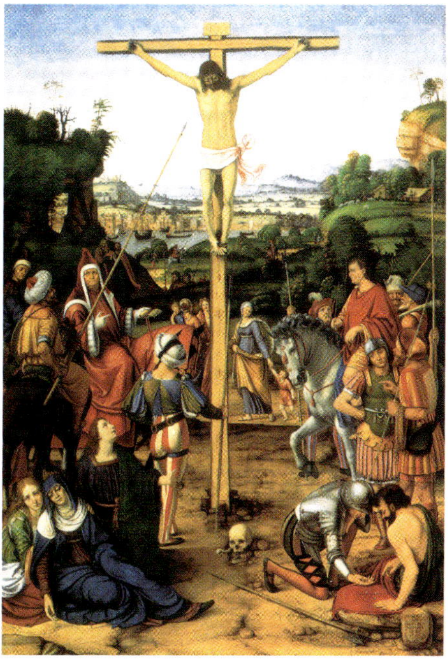

Andrea Solario, *Crucifixion,* c. 1503. Oil on canvas. Musée du Louvre, Paris.

Venetian influences slowly faded from his paintings to culminate in a *Crucifixion* (1503, Musée du Louvre, Paris), which is closer to the Lombard tradition and takes many cues from Leonardo.

Solario also applied lessons learned from Leonardo in his portraits, such as that of *Giovanni Cristoforo Longoni* (1505, National Gallery, London) and especially in his *Annunciation* (1506, Musée du Louvre, Paris) with its fine diaphanous outlines.

Although Solario had few commissions during the governments of the Sforzas (see Patrons), matters changed during the French occupation of Milan. Cardinal Georges d'Amboise called him to France* to decorate the chapel at Gaillon (which was later destroyed during the French Revolution). While in France he painted the famous, *Saint John the Baptist's Head* (1507) and a *Pièta,* both in the Louvre. In the latter, the figure of Saint John owes much to the angel in Leonardo's *Virgin of the Rocks.*

Upon returning to Milan in 1510, Solario was once again close to Leonardo.

In 1504, or thereabouts, he left briefly for Rome* where he may have painted an impressive *Cleopatra* (private collection, Milan).

After 1515 he remained in Milan and concentrated on large religious paintings and the portraits of dignitaries, which comprise a good portion of his later production. A fine example of the latter is *Gerolamo Morone* (private collection, Milan).

When he died he was working on three paintings on wood panels for an altarpiece, *Assumption of the Virgin* (Museo Certosa, Pavia).

SFUMATO

In the fifteenth century Leon Battista Alberti and Pierro della Francesca, as well as the Florentine neoplatonist* humanists, asserted the primacy of vision over the other senses. Their conclusions were based on mathematics as well as the consideration of light as both the vital principle of nature and the essential condition for its contemplation. As always, Leonardo considered both these approaches pragmatically. In order to understand space, Leonardo found it necessary to study the eye that perceives it. To understand light he studied reflection and shadow. He thus replaced intellectual symbols by observable phenomena, which opened up new areas of speculation. His consideration of spatial construction led him to find the perspective of geometrical linearity to be an arbitrary or at least an inadequate solution in comparison with the "spherical" or "natural" perspective he thought could more accurately describe three-dimensionality. His interest in aerial views, as evidenced in the background of his paintings, also increased over time. His most consistent problem relating to light concerned the rendering of contours and reflection at the same time. His invention of the *Sfumato* technique was the solution. Later, in the eighteenth century, Denis Diderot would explain *sfumato* as "a way of drowning contours in light steam." With *sfumato*, a sort of chiaroscuro technique, lines and edges are modified by applying light washes or glazing. This can render their more or less middle level tonalities darker or lighter, depending upon the effect desired. This hazy "light steam" is the visual manifestation of the constant, yet difficult to observe, work of water (see *Codex Leister*). This phenomenon was an obsession in Leonardo's thought and artistic practice. As the enemy of geometry, it blurs the sharpness of objects' definitions. As the enemy of permanence, it can impede and destroy any stable construction. As the enemy of heat and light it clouds the sun's rays. The problems of the mathematician and the physicist thus became a sort of protagonist in the painter's experimentation.

Perspective study for the *Adoration of the Magi.* Pen and ink and wash over metal point, 6 ½ × 11 ½ in. (16.5 × 29 cm). Galleria degli Uffizi, Gabinetto Disegni e Stampe, Florence.

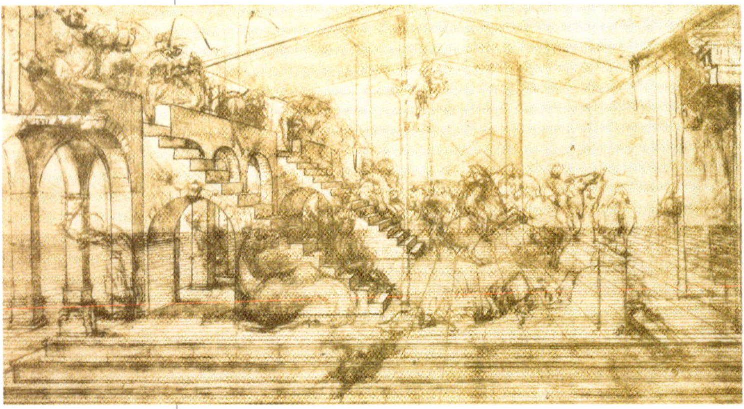

Stains and Inspiration

In this often-cited passage Leonardo proposes the most commonplace visual phenomena as sources of inspiration. Perception and imagination combine in an almost dream-like state: "I shall not refrain from including among the precepts a new aid to contemplation, which, although seemingly trivial and almost ridiculous, is none the less of great utility in arousing the mind to various inventions. And this is, if you look at any walls soiled with a variety of stains, or stones with variegated patterns, when you have to invent some location, you will therein be able to see a resemblance to various landscapes graced with mountains, rivers, rocks, trees, plains, great valleys and hills in many combinations. Or again, you will be able to see various battles and figures darting about, strange-looking faces and costumes, and an endless number of things which you can distill into finely-rendered forms. And what happens with regard to such walls and variegated stones is just as with the sound of bells, in whose peal you will find the name or word you care to imagine.

O painter, when you compose a narrative painting, do not draw the limbs on your figures with hard contours or it will happen to you as to many different painters who wish every little stroke of charcoal to be definitive. These kinds of painters well suppose that they will accumulate riches, but they will not acquire praise for their art for on many occasions the creature represented does not move his limbs in a manner that reflects the motions of the mind. When the painter has

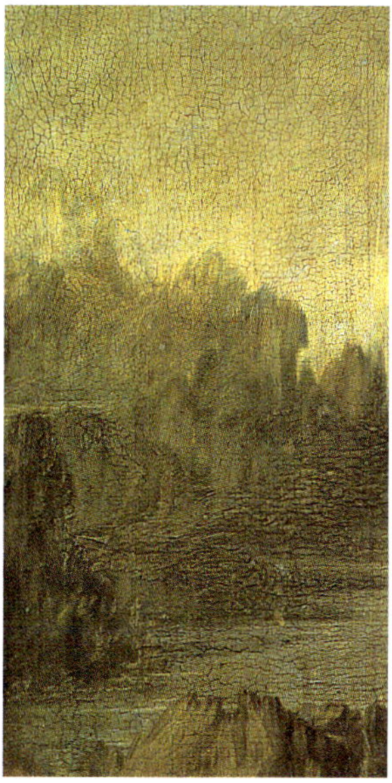

Mona Lisa (detail). Oil on wood panel. Musée du Louvre, Paris.

achieved a beautiful and graceful and well-defined rendering of these limbs, it seems to him an outrage to raise or lower the position of the limbs, or move them further back or forward, and these painters do not deserve any praise for their science.

Have you never reflected on the poets who in composing their verses are unrelenting in their pursuit of fine literature and think nothing of erasing some of these verses in order to improve them? Therefore, painter, decide broadly upon the position of the limbs of your figures and attend first to the movements appropriate to the mental attitudes of the creatures in your narrative rather than to the beauty and quality of their limbs.

You should understand that if such a rough composition turns out to be right for your intention, it will all the more satisfy in subsequently being adorned with the perfection suitable to all its parts. I have in the past seen in clouds and walls the stains which have inspired me to beautiful inventions of many things. These stains, while wholly in themselves deprived of perfection in any part did not lack perfection in regard to their movements or other actions." (*Codex A*, Institut de France, 102 v., Kemp, *Leonardo on Painting*, 222)

Theory

Few artists have more rigorously held that the visual arts are an intellectual enterprise than Leonardo. He insisted that the painter should be capable of constructing a coherent world based on a comprehensive understanding of natural causes and effects (see Art and Science). The fact that for him painting was the ultimate end of science makes it impossible to draw a line between his aesthetic and his scientific work. In Leonardo's earliest writings we find that many of his concerns were quite similar to those of his predecessor's in Florence* (see *Sfumato*). But the profundity of his thought and his great inventiveness enabled him not only to take their ideas to higher orders of elaboration, but also to put the fundamental bases of Quattrocento theories of invention and imitation, as defined by Leon Battista Alberti, into question. Thus his study of optics led him to conclude that the mathematical perspective, which his contemporaries depended upon, allowed for only schematic representations of what the eye sees and how it really perceives objects in space. In the tradition of fifteenth-century Florentine artists, the study of anatomy* was extremely important to Leonardo. But his desire to communicate action, thought, and emotion through the human figure was more detailed and profound. In his writings on the *paragone,** he argues for the superiority of painting over the arts of the ear (poetry and music) and over sculpture,* painting's main rival. Reading his writings on art one would think that he advocated an almost "photographic" sort of registration of nature and reality. But his paintings and drawings obviously exceed scrupulous scientific observation of the world. They are, above all, works of invention and imagination, where fantastic, mysterious, and ambiguous elements are always present.

Treatise on Painting

Leonardo had begun considering the project of a treatise on painting as early as 1490. The Institut de France's *Codex A* contains a draft. He continued compiling notes on the subject with the intention of eventually putting together a complete work. And although he refers to future publication in later manuscripts,* this never happened in his lifetime. After Leonardo's death, Francesco Melzi* enthusiastically sought to publish the treatise. He employed two copyists and got quite far in the effort, but did not accomplish the task. Melzi's compilation became the property of a Milanese painter mentioned by Vasari,* and then went to the library of the duke of Urbino before the Vatican acquired it in 1626. It is still in the Vatican collection and is known as the *Codex Urbinas (Latinus* 1270). This collection served as the basis for the first printed edition of 1651 of *The Treatise on Painting,* edited by

Paul Fréart de Chambray. Its importance is twofold: It was the only collection of writings by Leonardo accessible to the public before large-scale nineteenth-century philological studies of the manuscripts (see Historical Reception). It also offers a more or less intelligent selection of the author's writings on a number of topics no longer extant in the manuscripts as they come to us today. Yet it is incomplete and lacks organization. Entire chapters referred to by Leonardo, elsewhere in his notes, are missing. It also juxtaposes textual passages originally written at different points in time, joining together ideas in a manner that the author might not have agreed with. For these reasons, if Leonardo had an overall plan, it is not possible to discern it. According to the seventeenth-century art historian and critic, André Félibien, Nicolas Poussin, who illustrated the first edition, "did not believe we should have brought out this Treatise of Leonardo's, which in truth was disordered and not very well digested." (*Discussions* II, 1696) Martin Kemp has put together the most coherent English-language presentation of Leonard's writings on painting (see Bibliography).

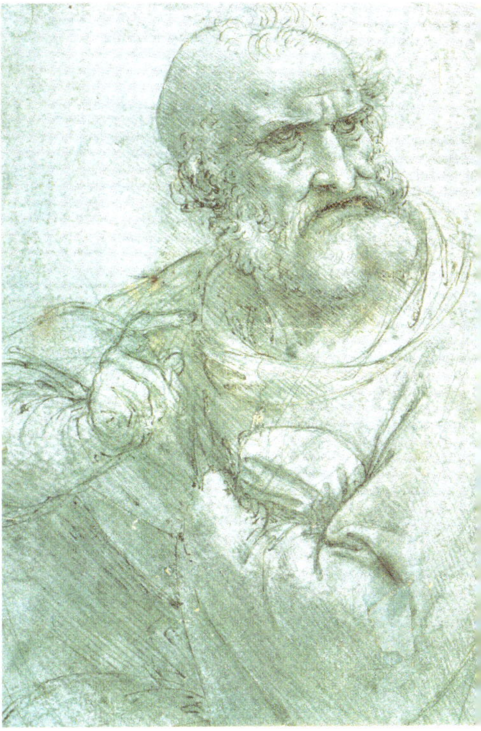

Study of Saint Peter for the *Last Supper*. Silver point, 5 ¾ × 4 ½ in. (14.4 × 11.3 cm). Albertina Collection, Vienna.

Vasari, Giorgio

Giorgio Vasari (1511–1574) was born in Arezzo and began studying in Florence* in 1524 with Andrea del Sarto, Micheangelo, and Fiorentino Rosso. He complemented his apprenticeship with trips to Rome* in 1532 and 1538 where he mainly studied the work of artists from the beginning of the century. Early on he put his talents for decoration into organizing large secular entertainments* and ceremonies, such as Charles V's triumphal entry into Rome in 1536, and he became a protégé of the Medici family. He painted numerous religious works, notably the decoration of the abbey of San Michele in Bosco, Bologna, and a famous *Immaculate Conception* (1541, Santi Apostoli, Florence) He traveled throughout Italy, contributing to the diffusion of second-generation Mannerism and coming into direct contact with most regional artistic schools. In 1542, he was in Venice* working on the decoration of a chamber in the Aretino; between 1542 and 1546 he was associated with the humanist circle of Cardinal Alessandro Farnese and decorated the Cancelleria in Rome with paintings in honor of Pope Paul III; from 1546 to 1554 he divided his time between stays in Tuscany, Romagna, and Rome. Cosimo I summoned him to Florence in

1554 and Vasari became the main agent of artistic policy for the archduke. Cosimo put him in charge of redecorating the Palazzo Vecchio (it was apparently at this time that the Leonardo's already damaged *Battle of Anghiari* disappeared) as well as the construction of the Galleria degli Uffizi and the creation of the Accademia del Disegno. His immense written work, *The Lives of the Most Eminent Painters, Sculptors, and Architects . . .* (second edition, 1568) is universally acknowledged as the founding work of modern historiography in art. It is still an indispensable reference for work in the field of Italian art despite a few lacunae, more or less minor mistakes, and the author's "Tuscan chauvinism." The biographies in his *Lives* are presented in three chronologically ordered stages representing the progression of the arts towards "absolute perfection." These stages were divided into that of Cimabue and Giotto; then Brunelleschi, Masaccio and Donatello; followed by that which begins with Leonardo and includes the "divine Michelangelo," for whom Vasari does not conceal his preference. Vasari does expressly state his admiration for Leonardo and gives some extremely fine readings of his works (see *Mona Lisa*), but he finds it necessary to reproach the artist for having spread his genius too thin and thus not completing more paintings.

Giorgio Vasari, *Studiolo di Francesco I*, 1570–73. Palazzo Vecchio, Florence.

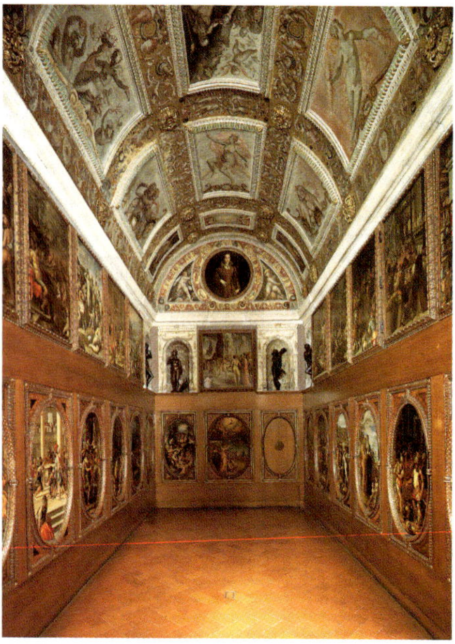

Venice

When Leonardo arrived in 1500, Venice had reached a turning point in its artistic history. During the first decades of the fifteenth century, Venetian culture was still predominantly international Gothic. As its possessions spread inland and its contact with the rest of Italy increased, so did its reputation as a humanist city. The most significant aspects of its humanist transformation were the publication of works by Ermolao Barbaro and Bernardo Bembo; Cardinal Bessarion's donation of a significant collection of ancient texts to the Biblioteca Marciana; and the establishment of Aldo Manuzio's press, which published classical texts in Greek and Latin. In painting, the genius of Giovanni Bellini—which should not occlude the contributions of artists such as Vivarini, Vittore Carpaccio, and Cima da Conegliano—fully assimilated the innovations of central Italy. Bellini then transcribed them into an extremely astute formal pictorial language in which light effects and chromatic finesse are put into the service of a tranquil pantheism. At the time, Venice presented the only credible

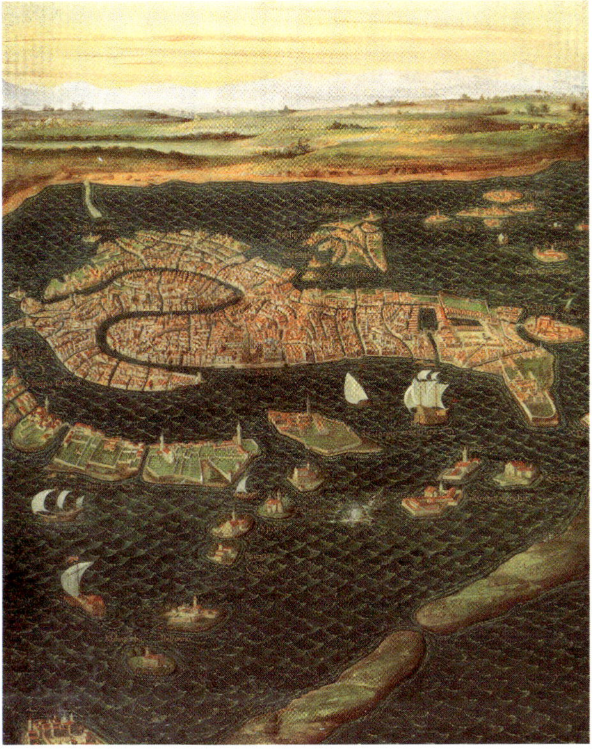

Ignazio Danti, *Venice*, 1580–81. Fresco, 10 ft. 2. × 4 ft. 11 in. (310 × 150 cm). Vatican, Galleria delle Carte Geografiche.

artistic alternative to Roman-Tuscan classicism. Giorgione's innovations broke completely with Quattrocento habits. His experiments were analogous to those of Leonardo and literally enthralled the younger Venetian generation. His innovations consisted in applying pigments directly to the canvas without preliminary sketching and sometimes even without applying an undercoating. This was the beginning of a new conception of painting—for the first time color was considered a means of autonomous expression. As with Leonardo, forms were not defined by outlines but with atmospheric effects and the pursuit of chromatic agreements in relation to dominant tones. Giorgione's approach was taken up by Titian and Sebastiano del Piombo. This solidified the contemporary and art historical distinction between Florentine "outlining" and Venetian "color" that Leonardo's painting endeavored to get beyond. As David Rosand has indicated, it is hard not to be struck by the many analogies between the techniques of Leonardo and Titian, particularly the use of their fingers in applying paint (see *Ginevra Benci* and *Saint John the Baptist*).

Verrocchio, Andrea del

Andrea del Verrocchio (1435–88) first trained as a goldsmith with Giuliano de' Verrocchi, about whom we know next to nothing. He learned sculpture in the workshop of Bernardo Rossellino, but also seems to have been much influenced by Desiderio da Settignano. It was from him that Verrocchio seems to have developed his penchants for naturalist experiments and the expressiveness of bodies and faces. His first known work, the *Funeral Monument to Piero and Giovanni de' Medici* (1470–72, church of San Lorenzo, Florence) still bears the marks of an artist accustomed to chasing reliquaries and precious cases with fine metals, but its abstract character and the absence of a human figure render it radically different from other works in the Florentine tradition. After this Verrocchio turned to more traditional subjects. A *David* (c. 1475, Museo Nazionale del Bargello, Florence) makes his debt to Donatello clear. After 1470 he turned to more emphasized naturalism. For example, Verrocchio originally conceived of his *Putto with a Dolphin* (c. 1478, Palazzo Vecchio, Florence) for a fountain, and locks of the putto's hair cling realistically to his forehead. His *Woman with a Bouquet* (c. 1478, Museo Nazionale del Bargello, Florence) is notable for how it escapes the rigidity of most Quattrocento torso-view portraits. And the famous *Incredulity of Thomas* (1467–83, church of Orsanmichele, Florence) presents a virtuoso articulation of the relationship between the figures and the space around them. Little is known of Verrocchio's oeuvre as a painter. Specialists have now assigned most paintings formerly attributed to him to other artists. His style, at least as far as can be made out from the portions of the *Baptism of Christ** attributable to him, seems comparable to Pollaiuolo and Botticelli; it is linear, dynamic, and intensely realistic with slight suggestions of Flemish touches. His *Virgin and Child with Saints John the Baptist and Zeno* for the Pistoia cathedral was completed by Lorenzo di Credi using principles associated with Leonardo rather than Verocchio, his master. Between 1485 and his death, Verrocchio was in Venice* working on the *Equestrian Monument to Bartolomeo Colleoni.* This masterpiece of expressive force and dynamism can still be seen on the campo San Giovanni e Paolo. Leonardo probably had it in mind when he was preparing the equestrian monument to Francesco Sforza (see Sculpture).

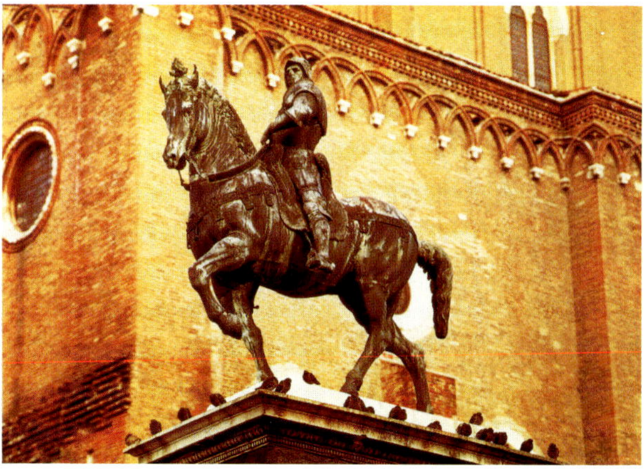

Andrea del Verrocchio, *Equestrian Monument to Bartolomeo Colleoni*, 1485–88. Bronze. Campo San Giovanni e Paolo, Venice.

Virgin and Child with Saint Anne and a Lamb

The *Virgin and Child with Saint Anne and a Lamb* (Musée du Louvre, Paris) is mentioned in the inventory of Leonardo's workshop* in Amboise in 1517. It became the property of Francesco Melzi* when Leonardo died, was returned to France in 1630, and has been exhibited in the Louvre since 1810. Despite the effects of imperfect restorations over time it should be considered a Leonardo original. Most critics date it to between 1510 and 1513. Like the *Burlington House Cartoon** it reveals Leonardo's intense contemplation of classical statuary, and his definitive abandonment of painting from nature in favor of compositions that adapt and refer to other artworks, without directly borrowing from them. It is an example of a frequent Renaissance practice, the Christianization of a classical scene. The homogeneous sculptural group of three figures is arranged similarly to the pyramidal configuration of the London cartoon, but the allusion to Christ's future sacrifice through the presence of the lamb is more explicit in the painting. The figures' postures and expressions are presented in such a way as to draw the viewer's attention to the speechless communication between the Virgin and her Son, under the melancholy gaze of Saint Anne. But the natural landscape, one of Leonardo's most fascinating and complicated, best reveals the perfection of his technique. When looking at the descriptive mountains, which appear through the mists in the background, the geological transformations due to water erosion seem to be taking place before one's very eyes. Leonardo makes use of every degree of density and lightness, from the minute and compact rendering of the rocky platform supporting the protagonists, to the transparent effects of the hazy mists in the distant background.

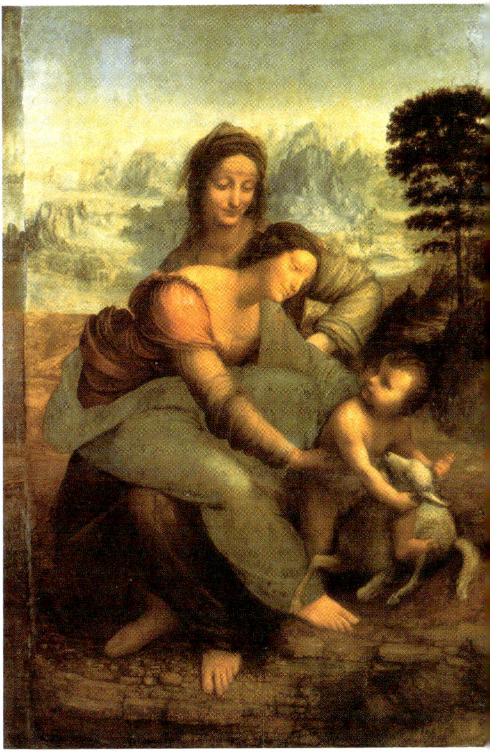

Virgin and Child with Saint Anne and a Lamb, c. 1510–13. Oil on wood panel, 5 ft. 6 3/8 × 4 ft. 3 1/4 in. (168.5 × 130 cm). Musée du Louvre, Paris.

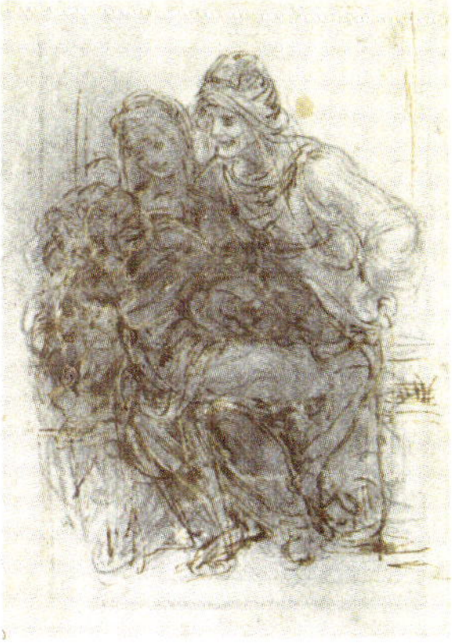

Study for *Virgin and Child with Saint Anne and a Lamb.* Pen and ink. Musée du Louvre, Graphic arts department, Paris.

VIRGIN OF THE ROCKS FIRST VERSION, PARIS

Leonardo and the de Predis* brothers were commissioned to paint "The Virgin with Child, Infant Saint John the Baptist, and Angel," now known as *the Virgin of the Rocks* (Musée du Louvre, Paris), on April 25, 1483. It was planned for the chapel of the Immaculate Conception in the church of San Francesco Grande, Milan. The work has always been attributed to Leonardo. Experts now agree that it was begun in 1483 and completed in 1486. Little is known of its itinerary before becoming part of the French royal collection, where the first reference to it was made in 1625. Another mysterious aspect is its composition, which is supposed to illustrate the theme of the Immaculate Conception. It does not help matters that the iconography of the figures is unclear and their expressions are ambiguous (as will be the case in many Leonardo paintings thereafter). The child Jesus has no halo and occupies a less important position than John the Baptist; the androgynous face of the angel seems at least partially inspired by classical sculptures of harpies; the natural décor also breaks with tradition; and the desert where John and Jesus are supposed to have met has been replaced with rocks, vegetation, and water. A theological debate on the Immaculate Conception had rocked Milan* in 1475. Pope Sixtus IV resolved the conflict by sanctioning a thesis, adopted by the Franciscans, whereby Mary was saved from original sin before even being conceived. But it seems that Leonardo took inspiration for his scene from the more or less heretical theory of Amadeo Mendes da Silva. For da Silva, the Old Testament prefigured not the coming of Jesus, but that of John the Baptist, and Mary was assimilated to *sophia*, perfect universal knowledge in classical philosophy. If this is the source of the iconography, it is understandable that the Franciscans would reject a painting that marginalized Christ and emphasized the other two figures. Apparently both parties agreed that the painting could appear elsewhere if a new version (that which is now in London) devoid of such ambiguities were executed for the Franciscans. From a purely artistic perspective, the Louvre version presents a first mature implementation of the fusion of human figures and a natural landscape that Leonardo frequently describes in his manuscripts.* The highlights and atmosphere reach a level of finesse and subtlety achieved by no other painter.

Virgin of the Rocks, c. 1483–86. Oil on wood panel, 6 ft. 6 × 4 ft. ½ in. (199 × 122 cm). Musée du Louvre, Paris.

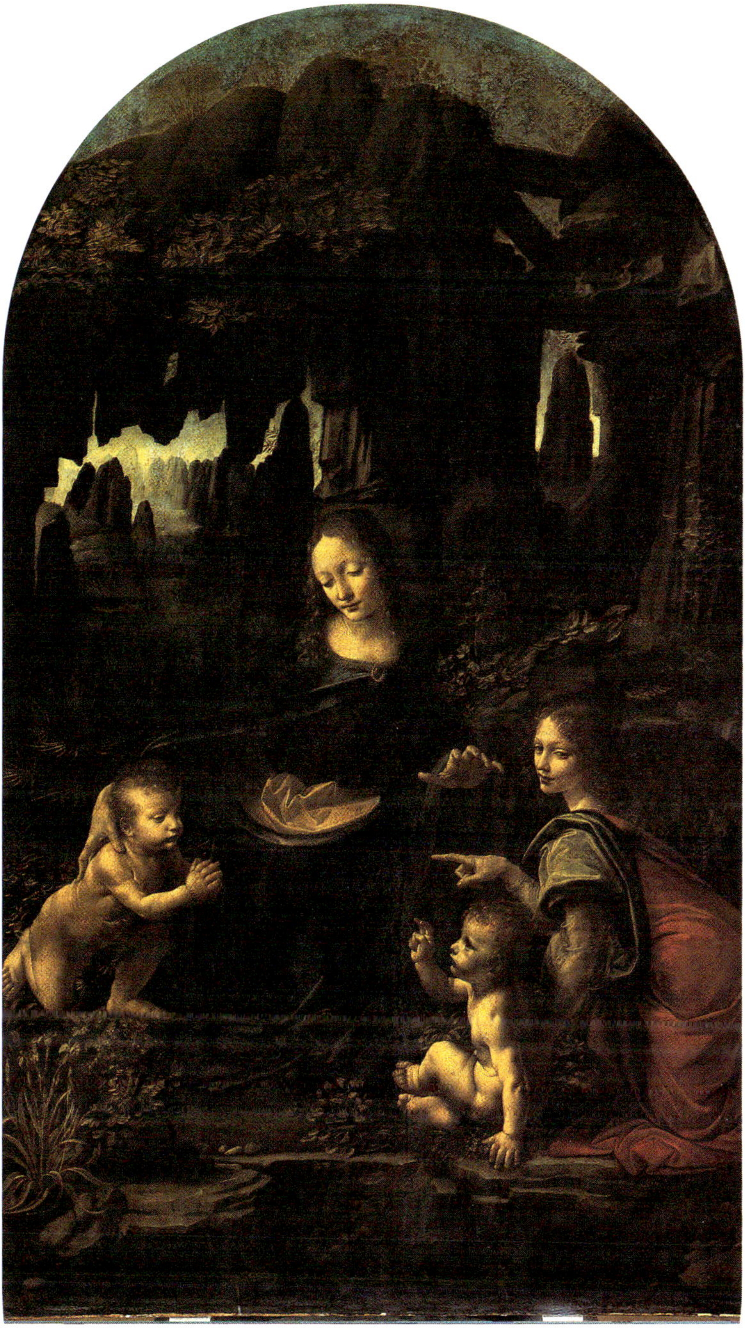

Happy is the estate which is seen by the eye of its lord.
This experience is proved,
that he who never puts his trust in a man
will never be deceived.

(*Codex Atlanticus*, 344 r., McCurdy, 60)

VIRGIN OF THE ROCKS SECOND VERSION, LONDON

It is known with certainty that this second version of the *Virgin of the Rocks,* now in the National Gallery, London, came from the church of San Francesco Grande in Milan.* Specialists attribute it either wholly or in part to Leonardo's studio with Leonardo's disciples, Marco d'Oggiono and Giovanni Antonio Boltraffio,* as the most frequently mentioned candidates for having worked on it. Execution is dated to between 1493 and 1508. Christ is now given a more central position in relation to the other protagonists in the scene. The figures occupy more space than before in relation to the landscape and the angel's ambiguous gesture towards John the Baptist has been eliminated, while the connection between Mary and her Son is reestablished in conformity with the wishes of the sponsors. Unlike the other painting, the Virgin now has a halo, as do Jesus and Saint John the Baptist, and the latter also now holds a gold cross. The message has been cleaned up and the protagonists are properly identified with recognizable attributes. And yet, these attributes may not be original elements of the painting. A copy that was made of the London painting between 1611 and 1614 (Pinacoteca Ambrosiana, Milan) contains neither haloes nor cross. This leads experts, such as Petro Marani, to believe that they are later additions. In any event, its greater monumentality and more naturalistic colors and light are evidence of the evolution of Leonardo's technique. But the question of the extent of Leonardo's participation in the execution must still be resolved. Paradoxically his presence is most amply seen in the incomplete portions, such as the rocks and the vegetation of the lower right side. The angel's left hand supporting Christ's back is definitely the work of Leonardo. And the flesh tones, particularly the skin of the Virgin and children's faces, bear traces of fingerprints, a means of handling the pictorial material already discernable in a few of Leonardo's early works. Scientific analyses have led to the following hypothesis concerning the painting's execution. After the panel had been prepared, Leonardo made a broad sketch of the composition with a brush, leaving the application of the colors to his students. Then Leonardo stepped in to correct certain areas, for example the position of the children's heads or the Virgin's shoulders, and applied final touches, including working in glazes with his fingers so as to obtain chiaroscuro nuances.

Virgin of the Rocks, c. 1493–1508. Oil on wood panel, 6 ft. 2 5/8 × 3 ft. 11 1/4 in. (189.5 × 120 cm). National Gallery, London.

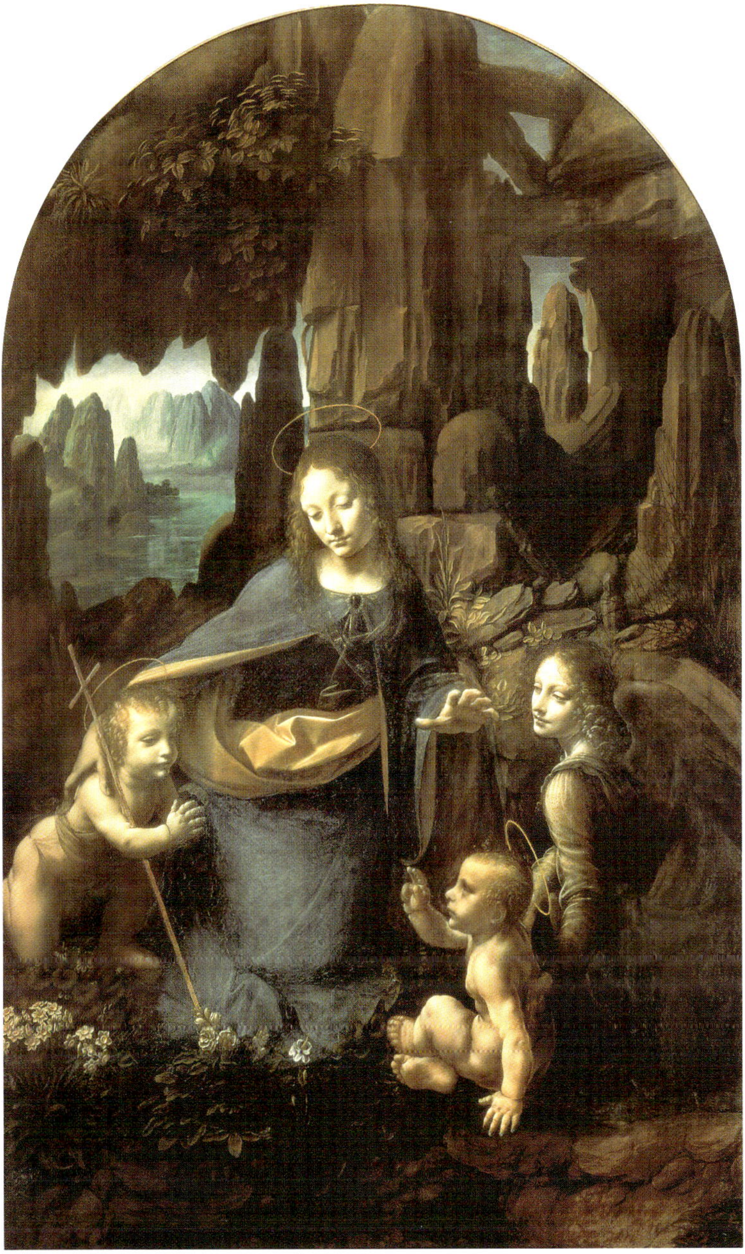

WORKSHOP

By observing nature in a purely analytical way, Leonardo discerned an aggregate of phenomena resulting from perpetually active forces. But when he went to work, he consistently found himself confronting the challenge of suspending the play of these metamorphoses, and of stopping the movement. His writings describe a series of ideal conditions for approaching this situation. They depend more upon the exigencies of pictorial representation than definitions of scientific truth. Leonardo considered painting the supreme form of knowledge and of art, the instrument of a fascinating and necessary illusion, which workshop activity had the task of revealing. Nothing was left to chance, and Leonardo's recommendations in the *Treatise on Painting** are extremely detailed. He considers dimensions, the positioning and lighting of a piece, choice of materials, technical devices, and mechanical procedures, which suggests that his workshop (also known as a *bottega*) was extremely well ordered, clean, silent, and active. Verrocchio's* workshop was one of the first to introduce the oil paint technique invented by the Flemish to Italy. Without it, Leonardo's experiments with transparent shadows, light glazes, and *sfumato** would have been inconceivable. Their importance is attested to by early sources, and particularly by Vasari,* although modern laboratory analyses of paintings still have not revealed all the mysteries of Leonardo's techniques. The precise roles and contributions of people in the workshop on any given project also remains mysterious. On the other side of the medallion, it should be recalled that Leonardo's disdaining of traditional methods and his desire to innovate at all costs led to some significant setbacks. One example is the loss of the *Battle of Anghiari,* a work that is only known today through studies and copies.

It is impossible to convey the fine draughtsmanship with which Leonardo depicted the soldiers' costumes, with their distinctive variations, or the helmet-crests and the other ornaments, not to speak of the incredible mastery that he displayed in the forms and lineaments of the horses which, with their bold spirit and muscles and shapely beauty, Leonardo portrayed better than any other artist.

(Vasari, Bull, I, 268)

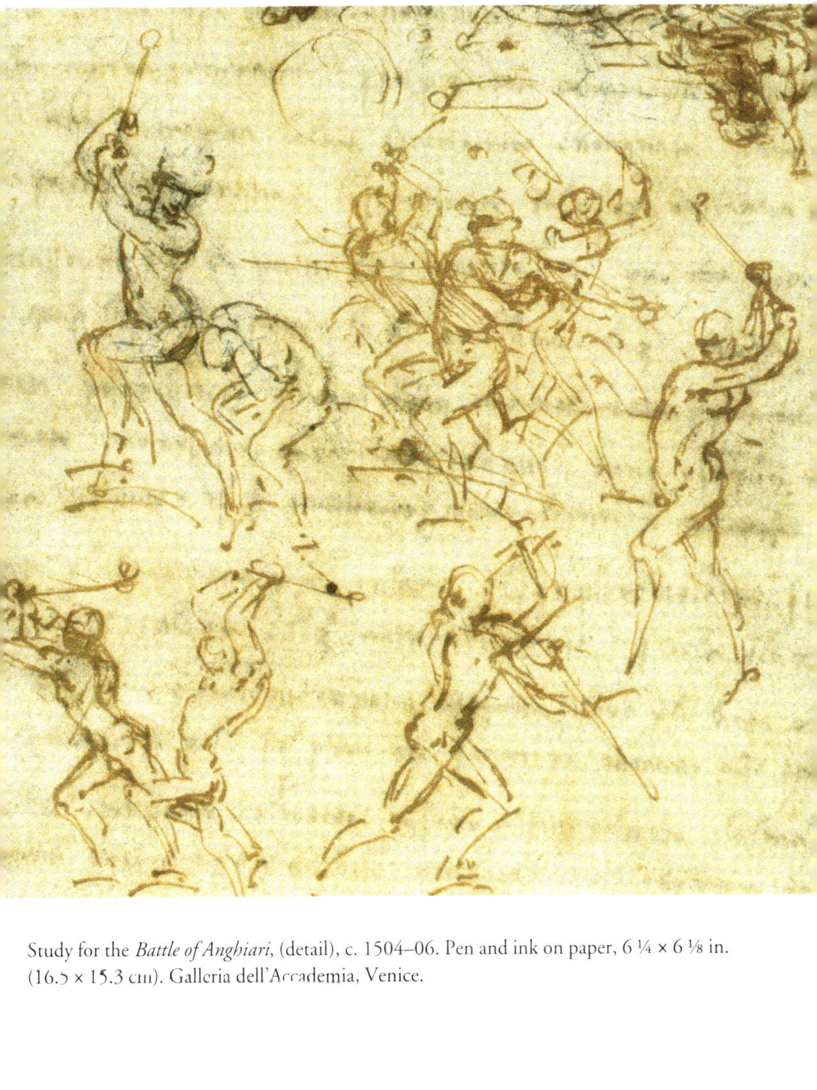

Study for the *Battle of Anghiari*, (detail), c. 1504–06. Pen and ink on paper, 6 ¼ × 6 ⅛ in. (16.5 × 15.3 cm). Galleria dell'Accademia, Venice.

C H R O N O

1452 April 15. Leonardo di ser Piero da Vinci, the son of the notary Piero di Antonio, is born in Anchiano, near Vinci.

c. 1469 Leonardo joins Verrocchio's workshop.

1472 He is registered as a master in the Florence painters' guild, the Company of St. Luke.

1473 August 15. Earliest dated work, *The Arno Valley* (Galleria degli Uffizi, Florence).

1476 Leonardo and several others are tried for sodomy. He is cleared of all charges.

1478 Altarpiece commission for the chapel of Saint Bernard in the Palazzo Vecchio.

1479 According to Anonimo Gaddiano, Leonardo works for Lorenzo the Magnificent.

1481 Contract for the *Adoration of the Magi*, commissioned by the monks of San Donato in Scopeto.

1482 Leaves for Milan where he is received at the court of Ludovico Sforza.

1483 April 25. The Franciscan monks of the Confraternita dell'Immacolata Concesione commision an altarpiece including the *Virgin of the Rocks.* He and Ambrogio de Predis sign the contract.

1487 Leonardo is paid for a project concerning the dome of the Milan cathedral.

1489 Leonardo organizes the entertainments for the wedding of Gian Galeazzo Sforza and Isabella of Aragon. Beginning of preparations for the great equestrian monument to Francesco Sforza.

1490 Design of a number of pageants and events, the most famous being for Bellincioni's *Festa del paradiso* on January 13.

1491 Gian Giacomo Caprotti da Oreno, aged ten, enters the service of Leonardo. Leonardo dubs him Salai, which means "demon" in Tuscan.

1492 Leonardo designs the procession costumes for the wedding of Ludovico Sforza and Beatrice d'Este.

1494 Irrigation, waterwheel, and farmland organization for the duke of Milan, near Vigevano.

1495 Leonardo begins the *Last Supper* as well as several works for the Castello Sforzesco.

1497 The duke of Milan pushes Leonardo to complete the *Last Supper,* which he does by the end of that year or the beginning of the next.

1498 Leonardo completes his murals in the Sala delle Asse of the Castello Sforzesco.

1499 Leonardo leaves Milan accompanied by the mathematician Luca Pacioli. He visits Francesco Melzi in Vaprio d'Adda, then stops in Mantua where he does the portrait of Isabella d'Este before heading to Venice.

1500 March, he arrives in Venice where he develops plans for defending the city from a Turkish attack. April, he returns to Florence.

1502 Leonardo enters the service of Cesare Borgia as an architect and military engineer and accompanies him on campaigns in northern and central Italy.

1503 Return to Florence. According to Vasari, it is at this point that he paints the *Mona Lisa* and *Leda and the Swan.* During the siege of Pisa, Leonardo develops projects for diverting the Arno River. The Florentine government commissions the *Battle of Anghiari.*

1504 Work continues on the *Battle of Anghiari.* Leonardo is called upon to be a member of the commission deciding on the installment of Michelangelo's *David.* July 9 his father dies.

1505 Called upon by the French government in Milan, he agrees to leave Florence for three months but stays on in Lombardy longer than planned.

1507 September, he returns to Florence where he takes legal action against his brothers over his father's estate.

L O G Y

1508 Leonardo takes his final leave of Florence. Now in Milan, he designs an elaborate residence for Charles d'Amboise and works on plans for an equestrian monument to Gian Giacomo Trivulzio.

1509 Geological and hydraulic studies in the valleys of Lombardy.

1510 He studies anatomy with Marcantonio Torre at the University of Padua. New projects for the Milan cathedral.

1513 Leonardo leaves Milan for Rome where he stays under the protection of Cardinal Giuliano de' Medici in the Vatican Belvedere. His assistants Salai, Francesco Melzi, Lorenzo, and Fanfoia accompany him.

1514 Projects for draining marshlands and for the Civitavecchia port.

1517 Leonardo, accompanied by Francesco Melzi, is received at the court of Francis I in Amboise. He is lodged at Cloux near the French king's royal residence and obtains the title of First Painter of the King. Visited by Cardinal Luigi d'Aragona.

1518 He participates in the dauphin's baptismal ceremony and the wedding of Lorenzo de' Medici with the king's niece.

1519 April 23, Leonardo da Vinci drafts his last will. He names Melzi his executor and leaves him all manuscripts and works currently in his studio. Leonardo dies on May 2.

SELECTED BIBLIOGRAPHY

Monographs

Arasse, Daniel. *Leonardo da Vinci: the Rhythm of the World.* New York: Konecky & Konecky, 1998.

Clark, Kenneth. *Leonardo da Vinci: An Account of his Development as an Artist,* (1939). Revised and edited by Martin Kemp. London: Viking, 1988.

Marani, Pietro C. *Leonardo da Vinci: the Complete Paintings.* Translated by. A. Lawrence Jenkins. New York: Harry N. Abrams, 2000.

Wasserman, Jack. *Leonardo da Vinci.* New York: Harry N. Abrams, 1975.

Studies and Biographies

Brambilla Barcilon, Pinin, and Pietro C. Marani. *Leonardo: The Last Supper.* Translated by Harlow Tighe. Chicago: University of Chicago Press, 2001.

Brown, David Alan. *Leonardo da Vinci: Origins of a Genius.* New Haven: Yale University Press, 1988.

Rosand, David. *The Meaning of the Mark: Leonardo and Titian.* Lawrence, Kansas: Spencer Museum/Universtiy of Kansas, 1988.

Sassoon, Don. *Mona Lisa: The History of the World's Most Famous Painting.* London: Harper Collins, 2001.

Vasari, Giorgio. *Lives of the Artists,* a selection translated by George Bull. Rev. ed. 2 vols. London: Penguin Books, 1987.

White, Michael. *Leonardo the First Scientist.* New York: St. Martin's Press, 2000.

Writings of Leonardo da Vinci

Chastel, André, ed. *The Genius of Leonardo da Vinci.* New York: Orion Press 1961.

Kemp, Martin, ed. *Leonardo on Painting.* Translated by Martin Kemp and Margaret Walker. New Haven: Yale University Press, 1989.

McCurdy, Edward A., ed. *Leonardo Da Vinci's Notebooks.* New York: Empire State Books, 1923.

Richter, Irma A., ed. *Leonardo da Vinci.* Cambridge: Oxford University Press, 1998.

Internet References

Kemp, Martin. "Leonardo da Vinci," *The Grove Dictionary of Art Online,* <http://www.groveart.com>

Richter, Jean Paul, ed. *Notebooks of Leonardo da Vinci* (complete). Translated by R C. Bell and E. J. Poynter. Project Gutenberg Release #5000. <http://digital.library.upenn.edu/webbin/gutbook/lookup?num=5000>

Quotes taken from this edition are indicated by the editor's name and the number that he assigned to the original manuscript, for example: (*Codex Atlanticus,* 170 r., Richter, 842).

INDEX

Photographic credits: AKG 6, 11, 12, 14–15, 16, 18, 19, 21, 22, 26, 27, 33, 34, 53, 78, 88, 90, 107, 115; Bridgeman–Giraudon 4–5, 7, 8, 24, 28–29, 38, 43, 45, 46, 47 top, 49, 50, 51 top, 51 bottom, 54, 57, 58, 66, 67, 72–73, 74, 79, 84, 86, 92 top, 92 bottom, 99, 100, 102, 105, 108, 113; Czartoryski Muzeum, Krakow 71; Electra Archives, Milan 98; Flammarion archives, 81, 93; National Gallery of Art, Washington 56, 60, 62; Réunion des musées nationaux 30 bottom, 31, 35, 44, 55, 59, 65, 83, 91, 94, 97, 109 top, 109 bottom, 111 / M. Bellot 61 / G. Blot: 23, 48 bottom, 76, 101, 103 / C. Jean 36, 40, 69 / H. Lewandowski 30 top/ Le Mage 48 top / R. G. Ojeda 13, 25; Scala, Florence 1, 41, 77, 106; Victoria and Albert Museum Picture 47 bottom; Windsor Royal Library 63.

Title page: *Vitruvian Man.* Pen and ink on paper, 13 ½ × 9 ⅝ in (34.4 × 24.5 cm). Galleria dell'Academia, Venice.

Pages 4–5: *Last Supper,* 1494–98 (after restoration). Tempera and oil on two preparatory layers, 13 ft. 10 × 29 ft. 7 ½ in. (4.6 × 8.8 m). Santa Maria delle Grazie, Milan.

Translated and adapted from the French by Chet Wiener
Copy-editing: Christine Schultz-Touge
Typesetting: Studio X-Acte
Color Separation: Pollina, S.A., France

ISBN: 2-0801-1136-1
FA1136-02-X
Dépot légal: 10/2002
Printed and bound by Pollina S.A., France - n° L88175